The Paintbrush Dreamer

by Wende Essrow

ROCK - PAPER - [SAFETY] SCISSORS

Buffalo, New York

Rock, Paper, Safety Scissors, 2495 Main Street, Suite 429a, Buffalo, NY 14214

publisher@rockpapersafetyscissors.com

Text and Paintings by Wende Essrow

Book Design by Mark D. Donnelly, Ph.D.

Soft cover: 978-0-9848787-5-8

Hard cover: 978-0-9848787-6-5

Printed in the United States of America

10 9 8 7 6 5 4 3 2 1

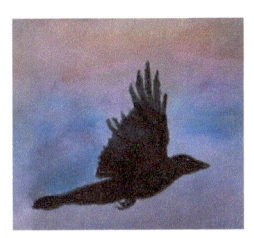

To all young artists:
"Walk with me in the morning sun as the
ravens fly up over the hills, and let all the
colors of the new day fill your heart."

Introduction:

When I was a little girl my parents gave me a birthday present that changed my life. It was a tin paintbox with a picture of a sailboat on the cover. I have been painting ever since that day.

A friend of mine calls me the "beauty hunter" and that is a good way to describe why I paint. Painting is my way of noticing and celebrating the beauty I see in nature.

My paintbrush is quietly saying "thank you" for all I see.

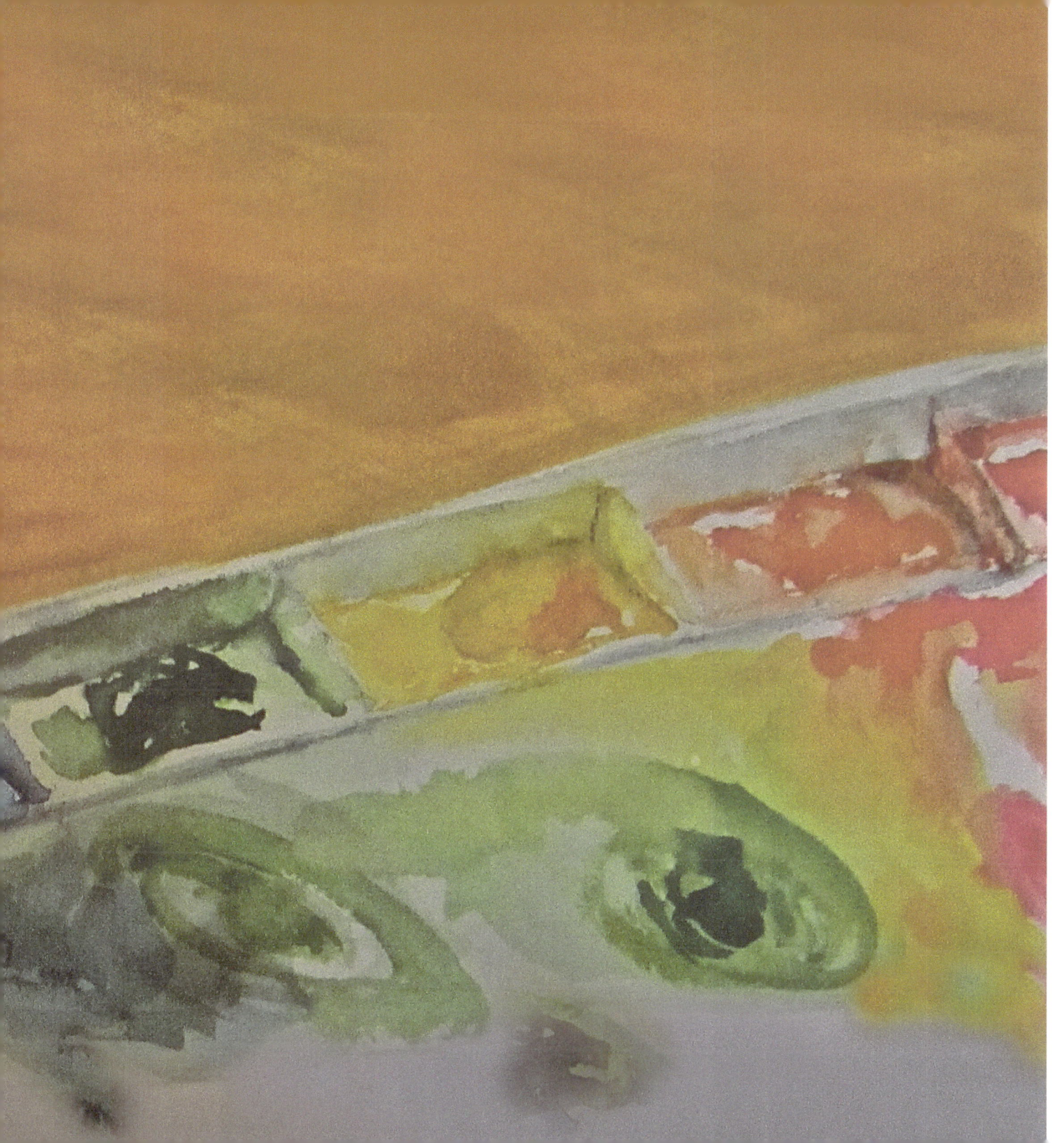

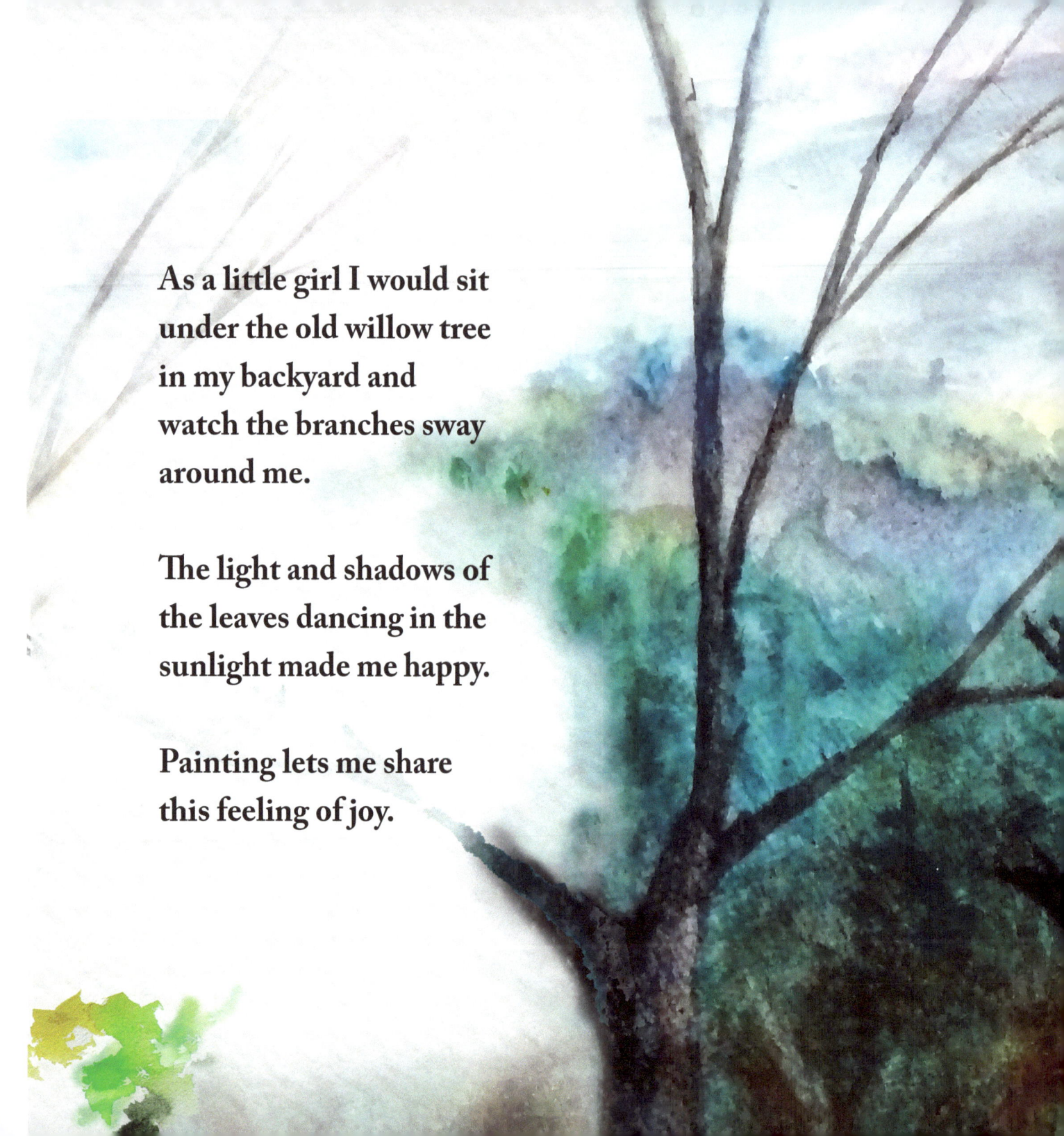

As a little girl I would sit
under the old willow tree
in my backyard and
watch the branches sway
around me.

The light and shadows of
the leaves dancing in the
sunlight made me happy.

Painting lets me share
this feeling of joy.

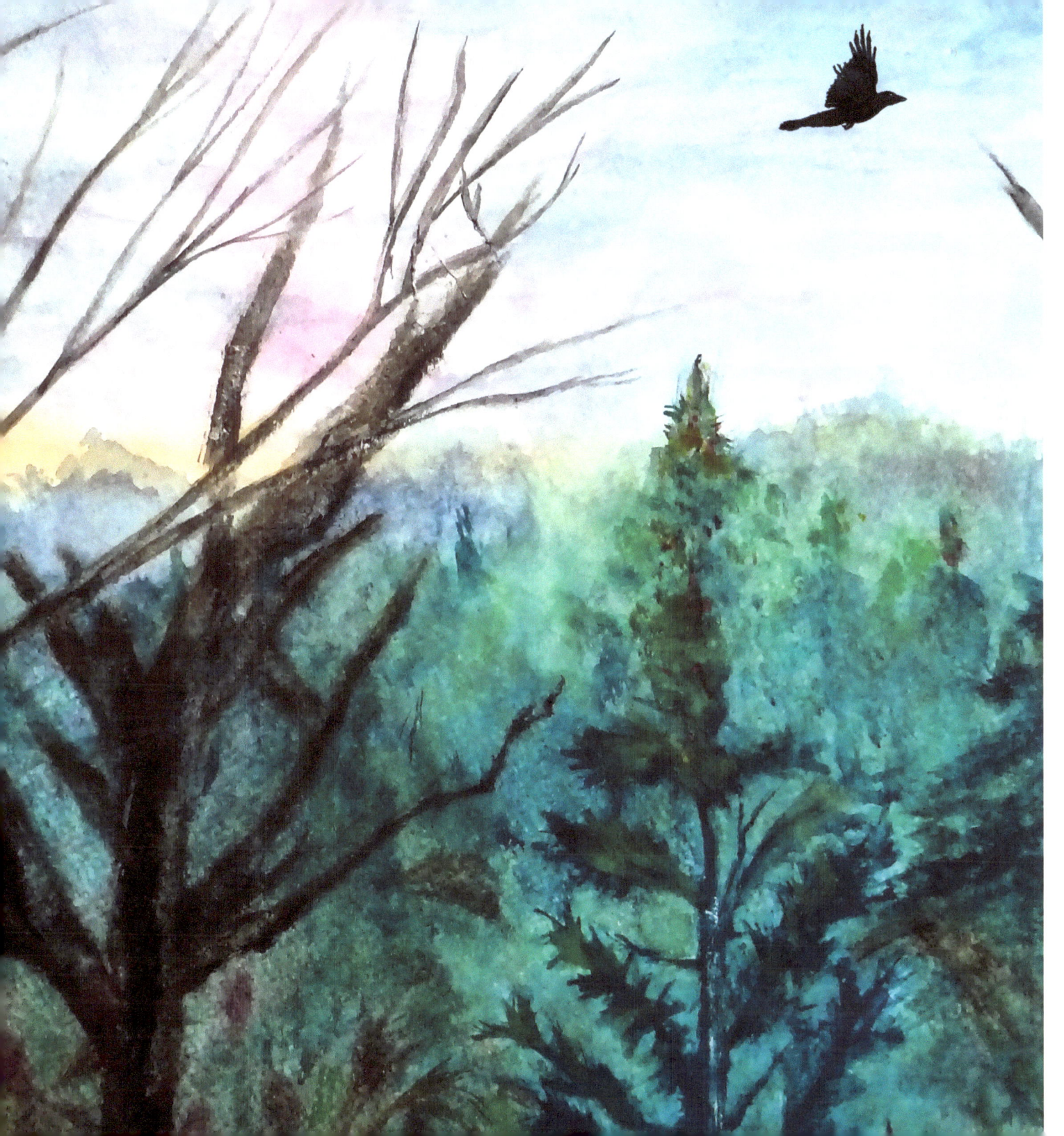

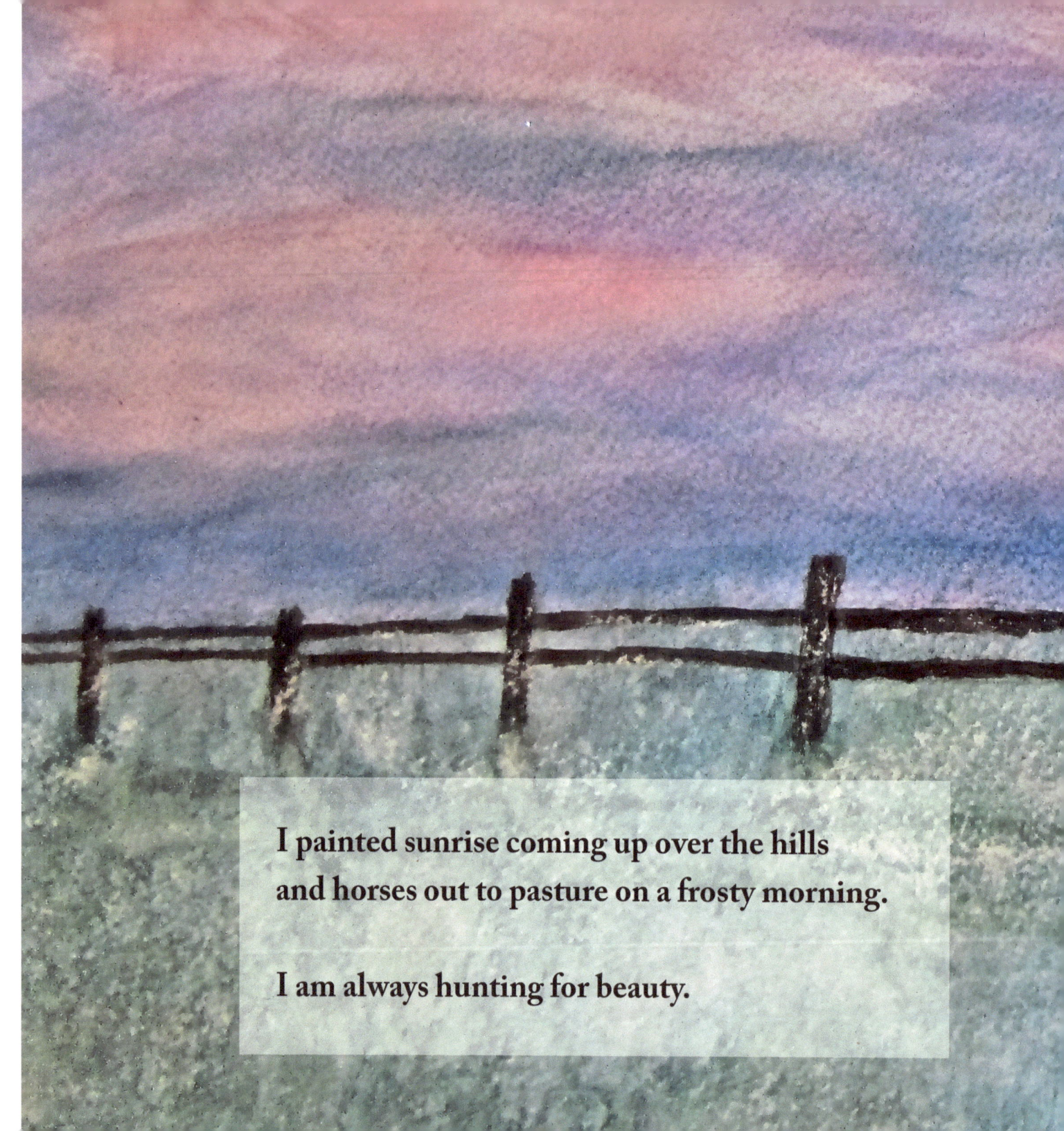

I painted sunrise coming up over the hills
and horses out to pasture on a frosty morning.

I am always hunting for beauty.

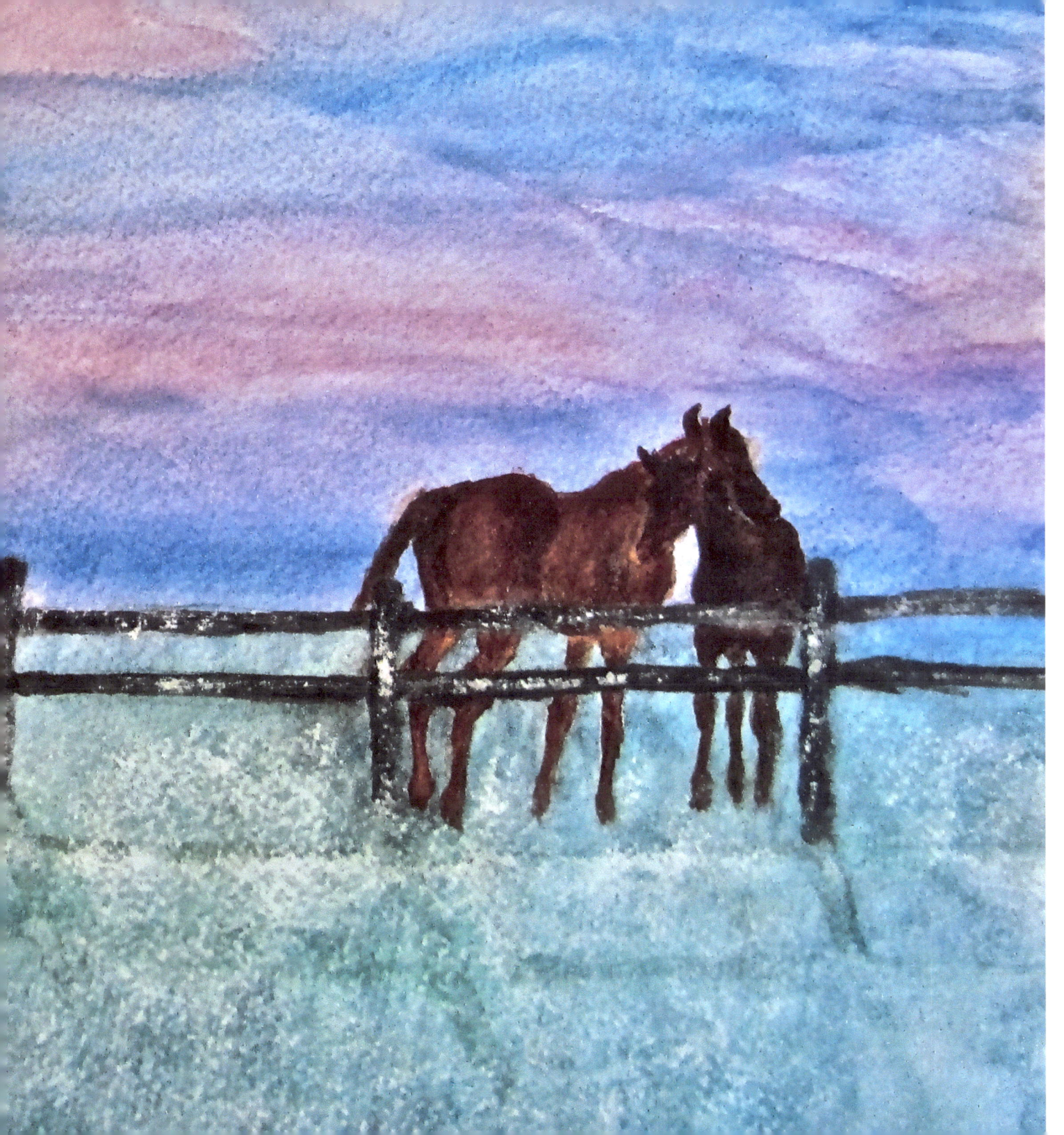

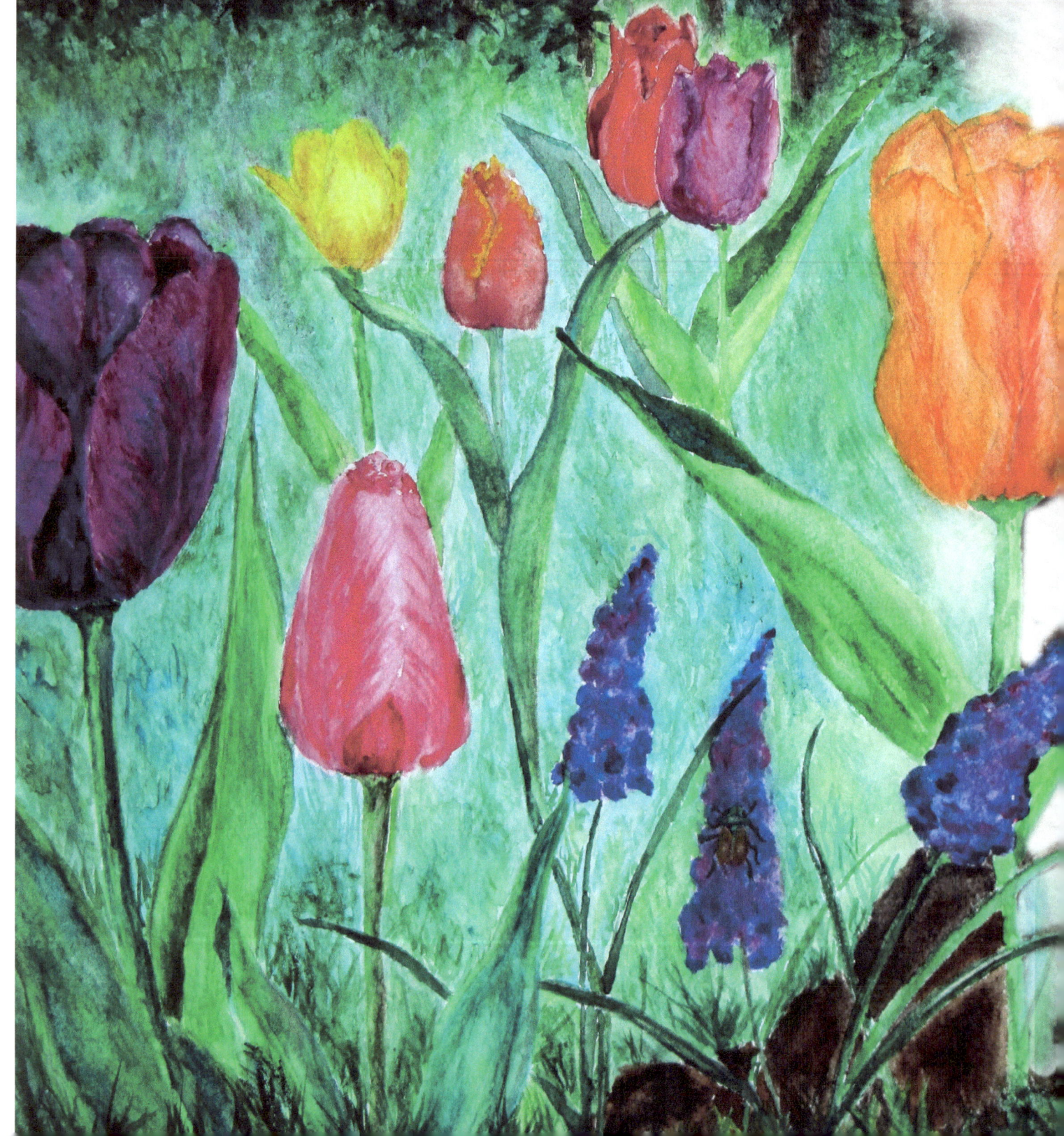

I take paint, paper, brushes, and a jar of water
and search for birds, animals, and flowers.

Now I begin to paint.

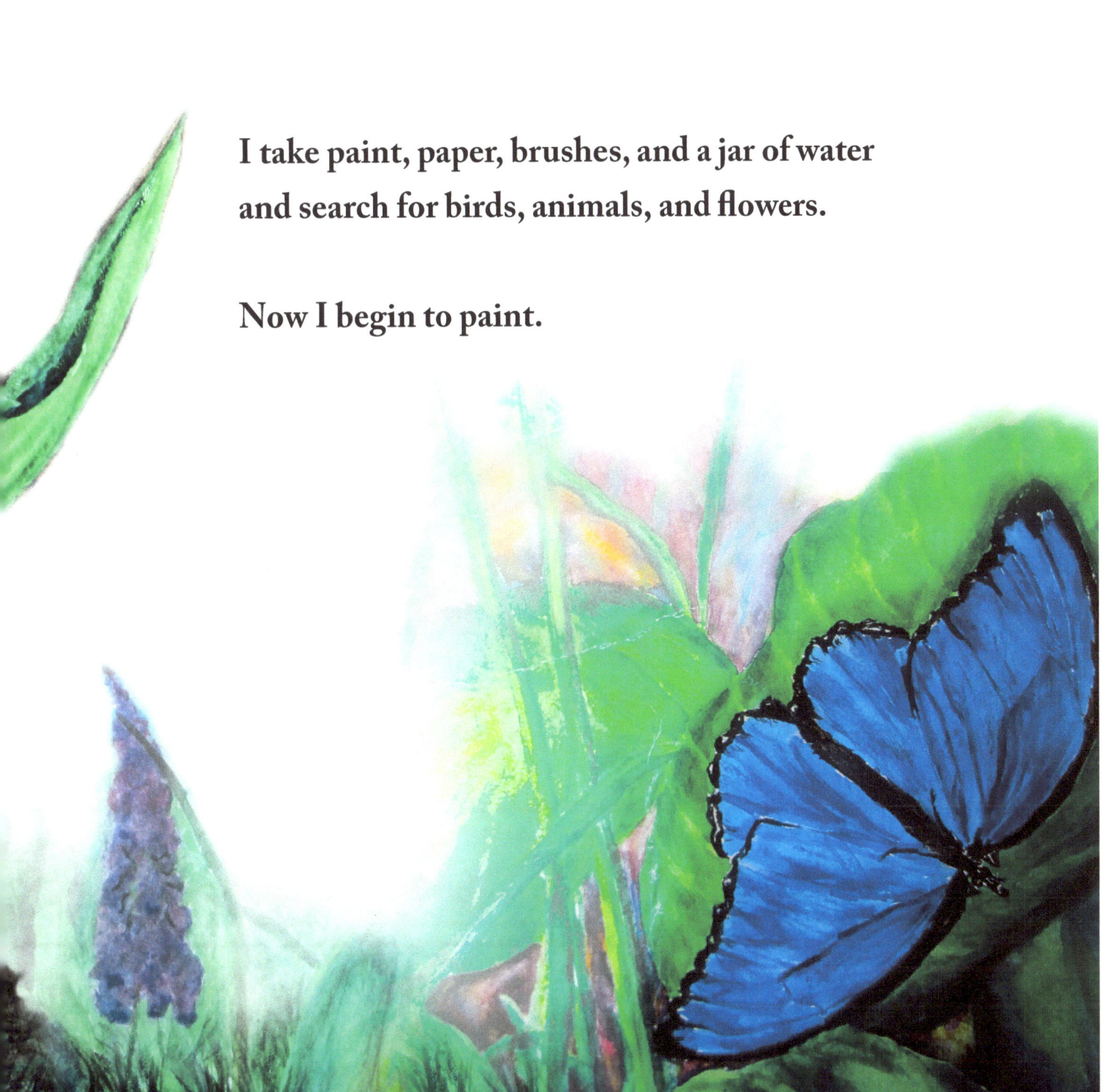

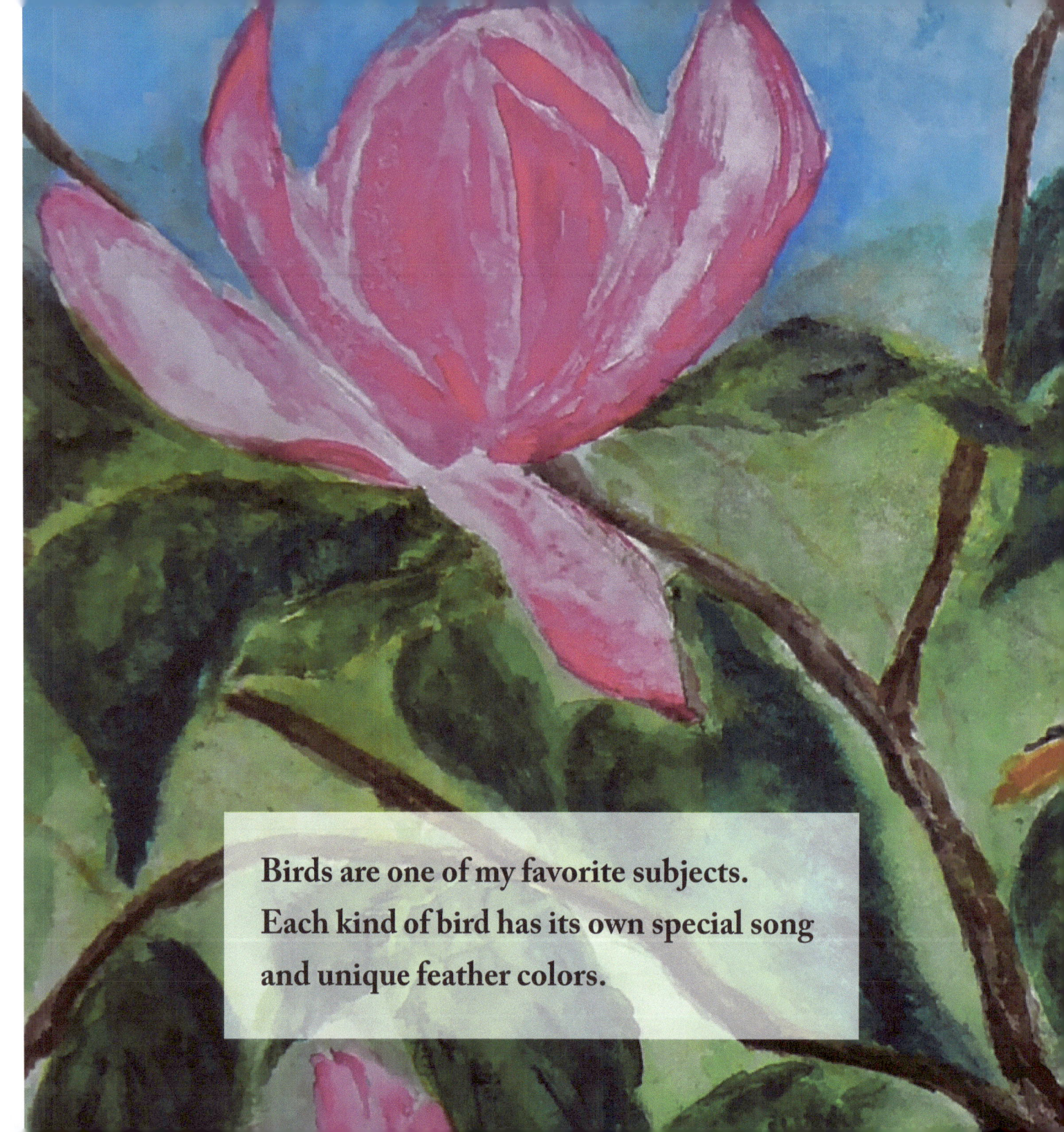

Birds are one of my favorite subjects.
Each kind of bird has its own special song
and unique feather colors.

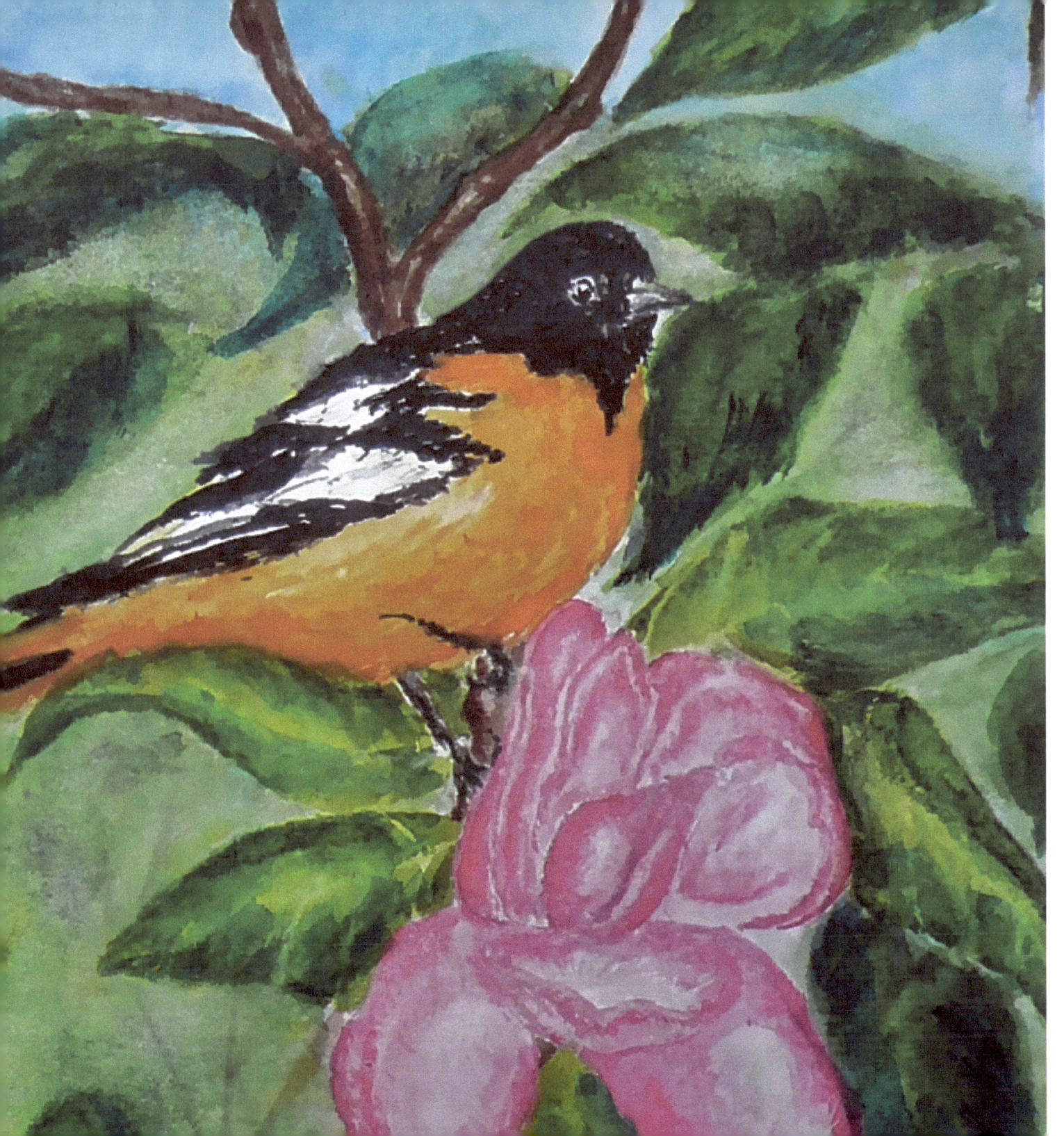

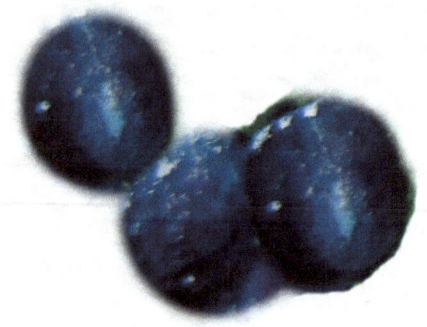

I wished with all my heart to live in a house in the woods where I would paint the many different colored birds of the forest.

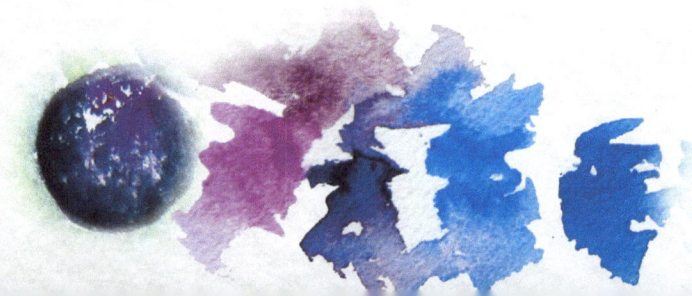

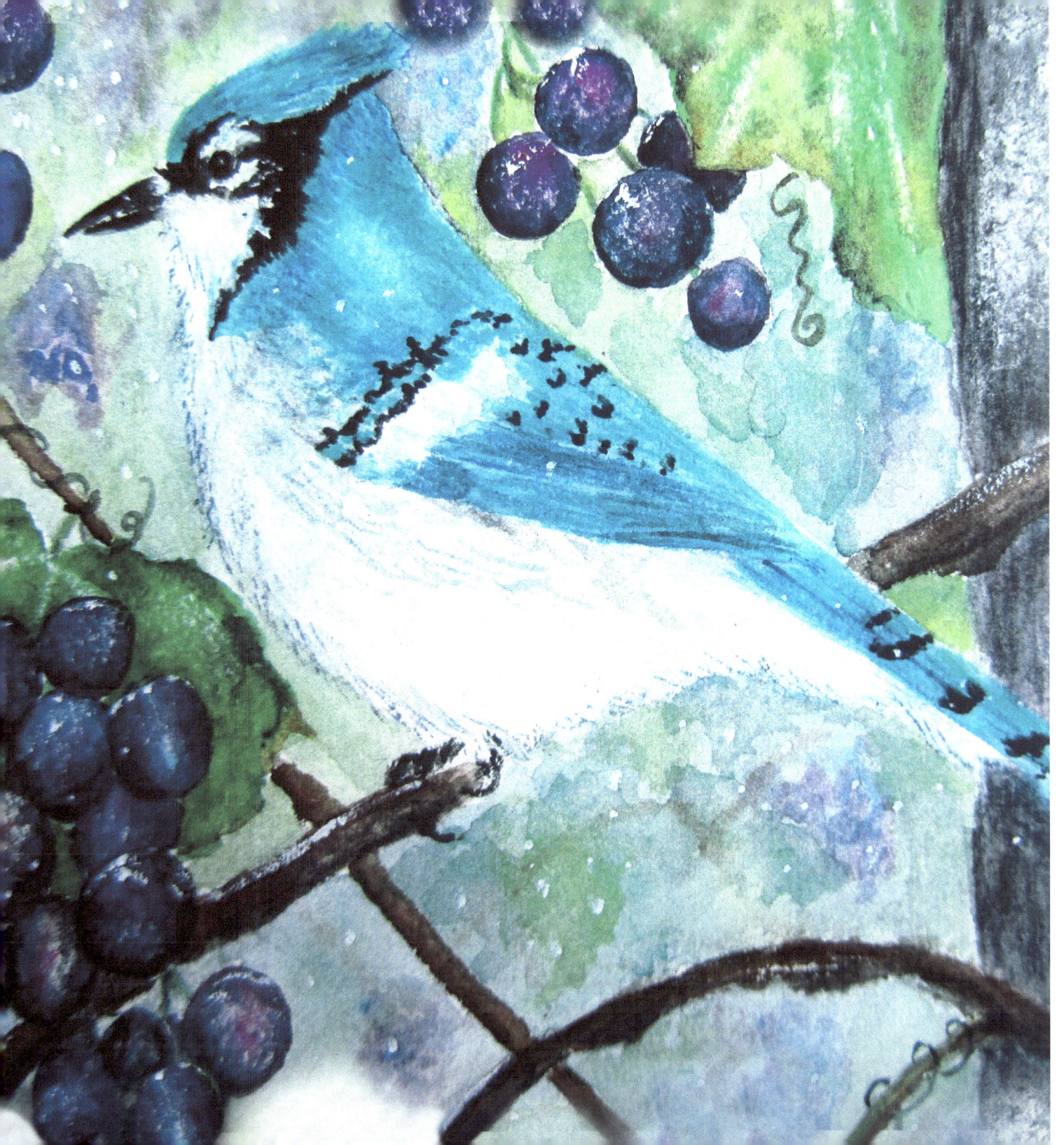

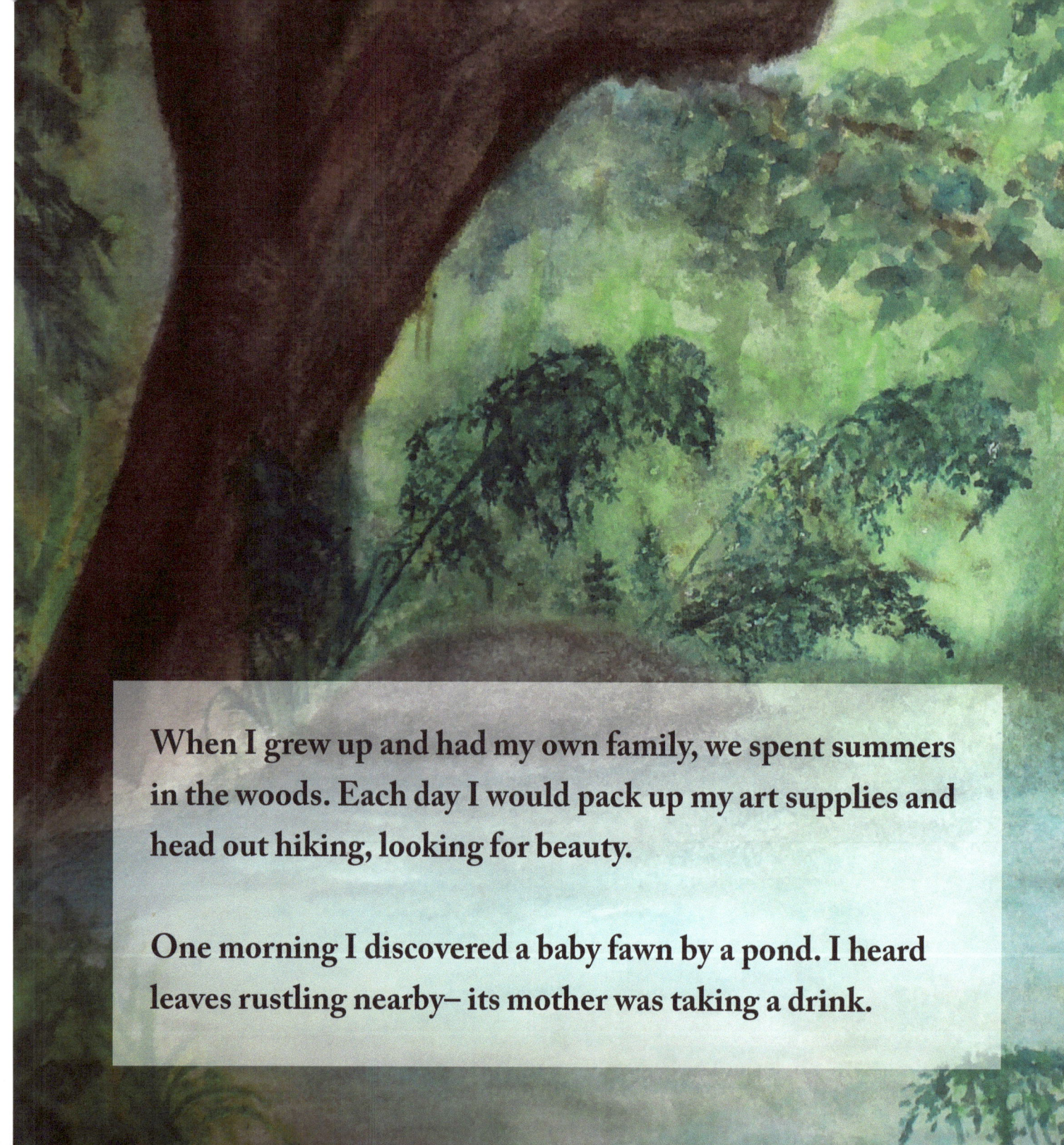

When I grew up and had my own family, we spent summers in the woods. Each day I would pack up my art supplies and head out hiking, looking for beauty.

One morning I discovered a baby fawn by a pond. I heard leaves rustling nearby– its mother was taking a drink.

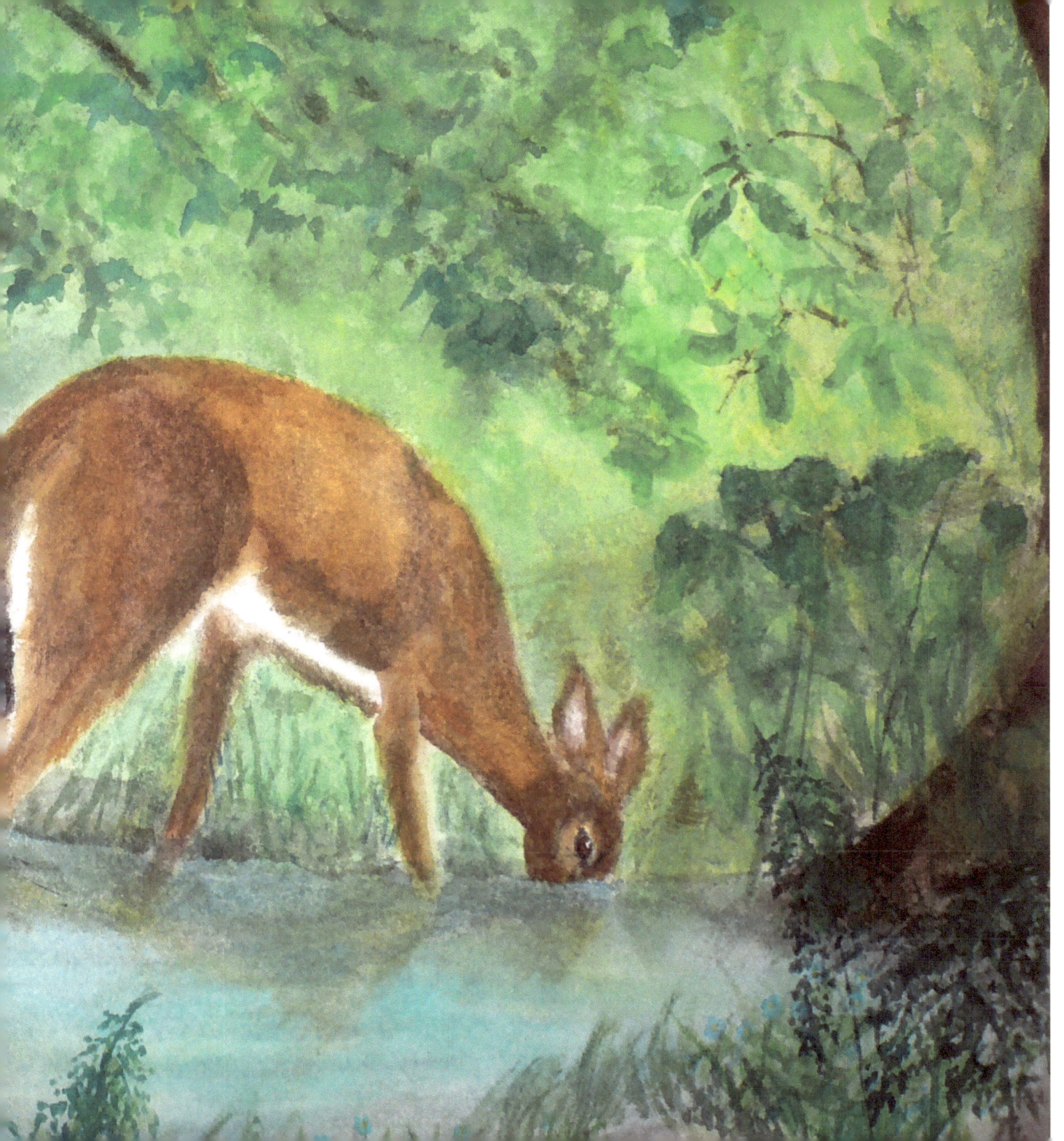

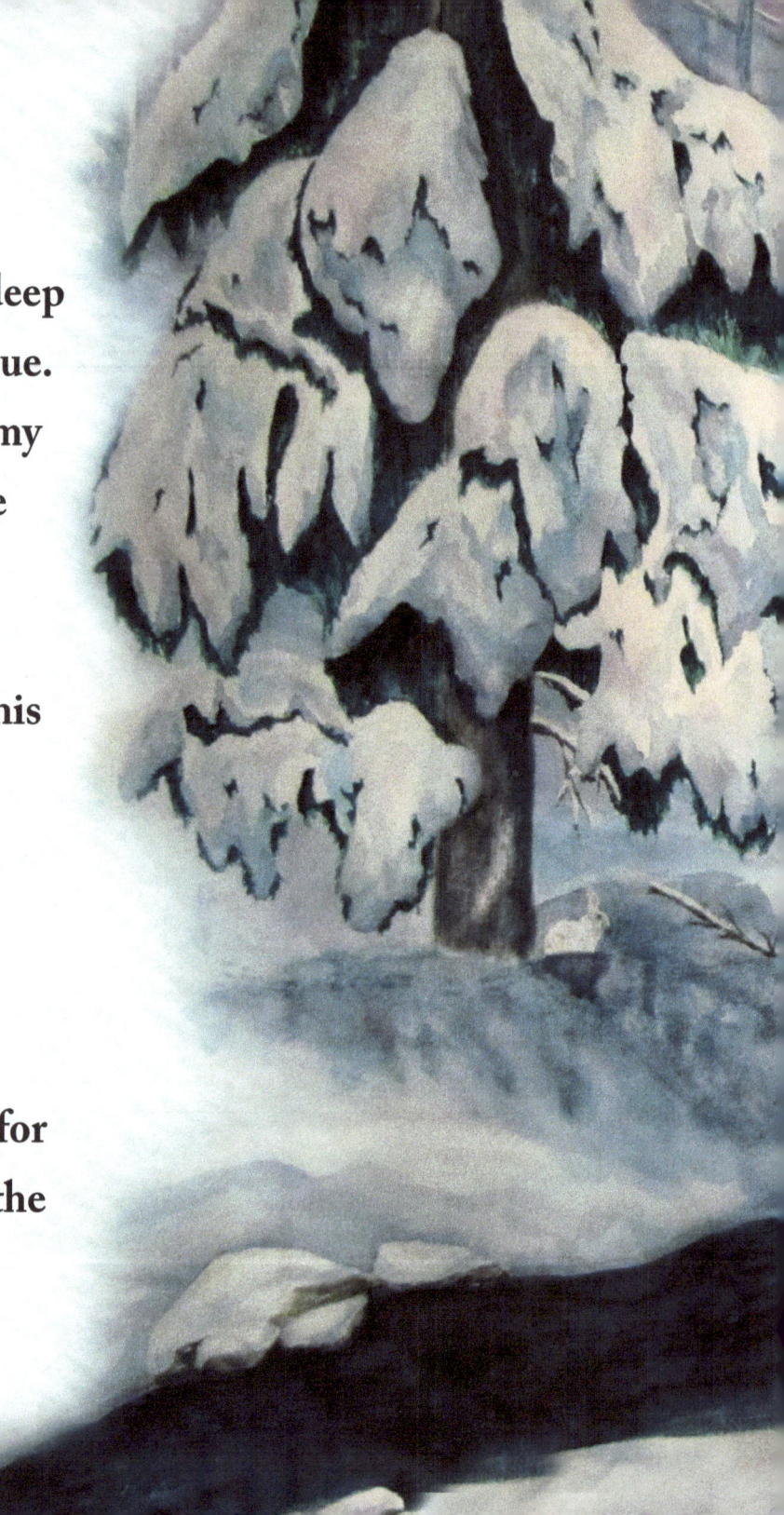

My dream of an art studio deep in the woods finally came true. The view of the creek from my studio window is exactly the same as in this painting.

But guess what? I painted this ten years before my dream came true!

My paintbrush knew.

Is there one thing you wish for more than anything else in the whole world?

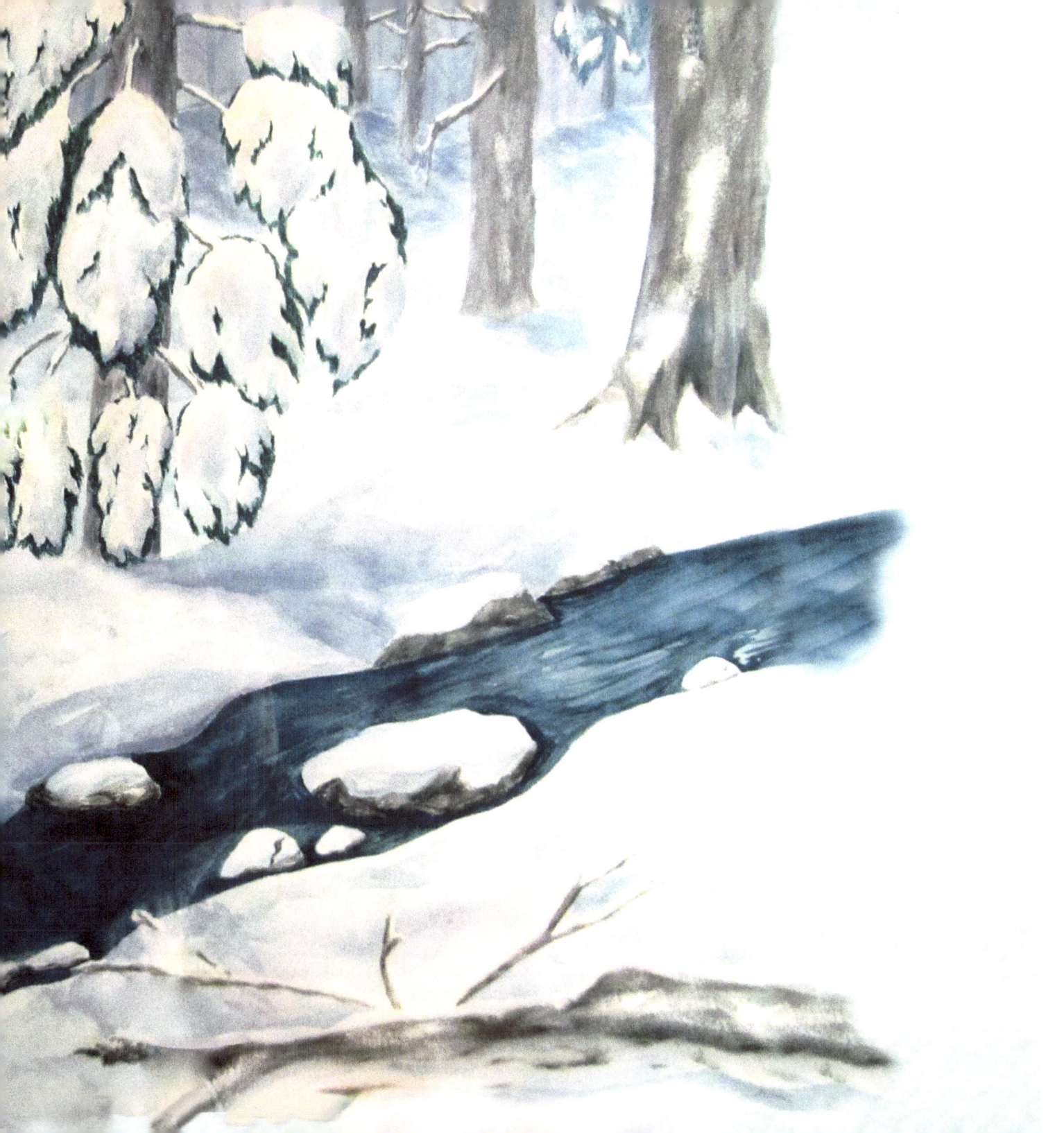

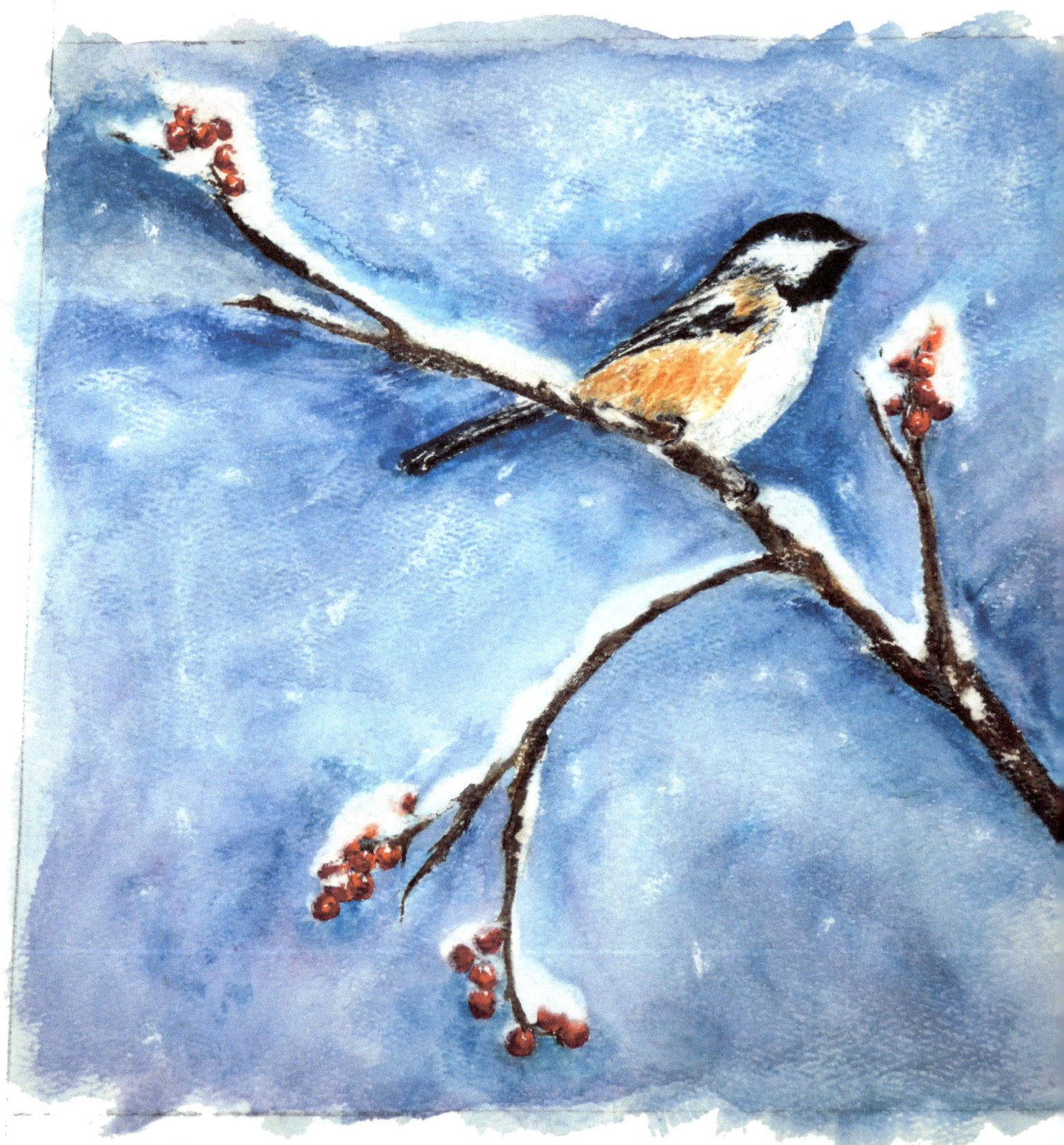

Now that I live in the forest there are so many lovely things to paint. This chickadee visits outside my studio window.

I leave birdseed out and many feathered friends stop by on chilly winter days.

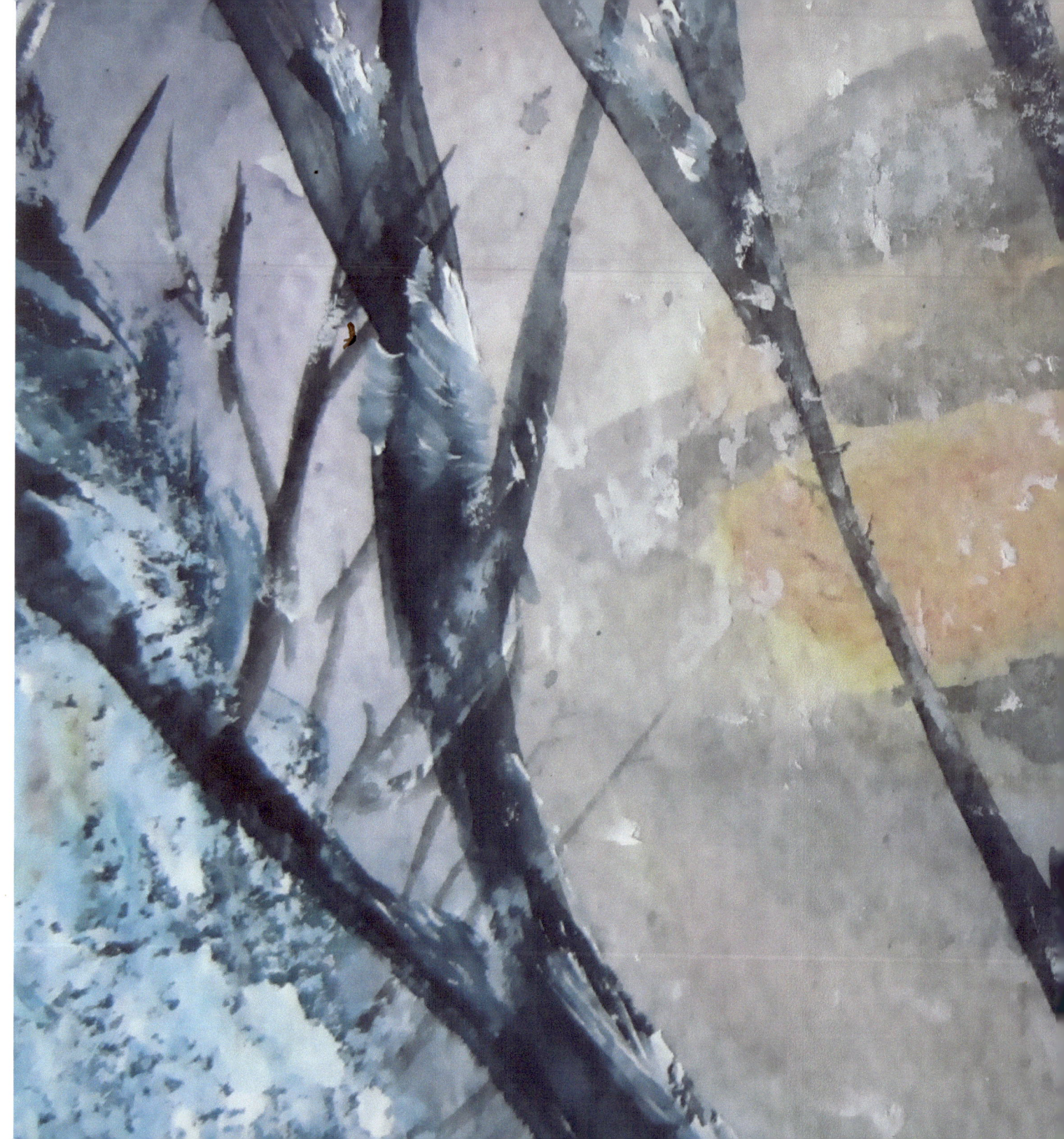

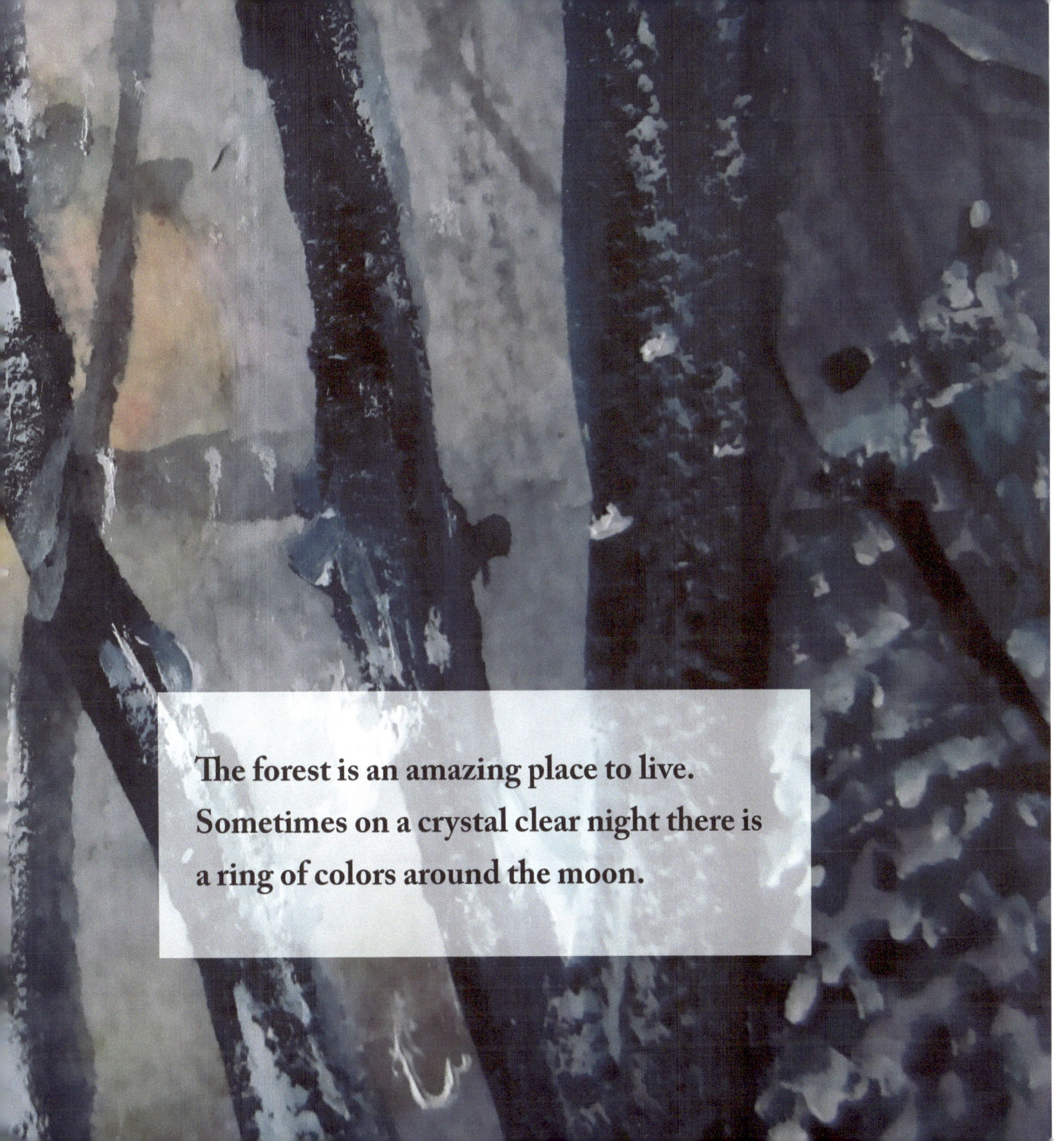

The forest is an amazing place to live.
Sometimes on a crystal clear night there is
a ring of colors around the moon.

I hear an owl in the treetops and begin to imagine how I will paint him someday.

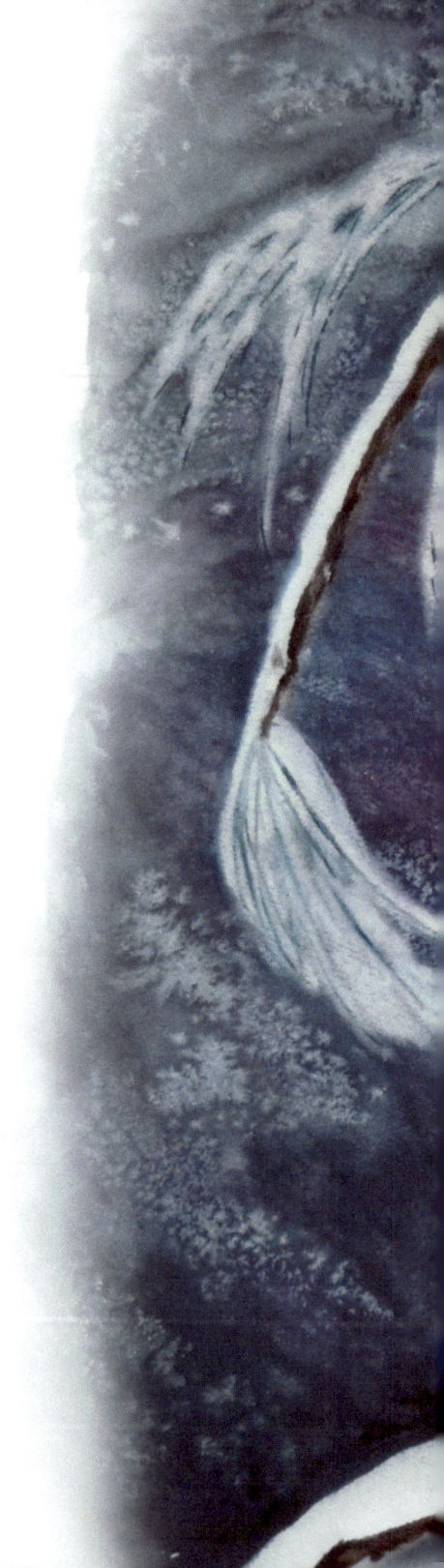

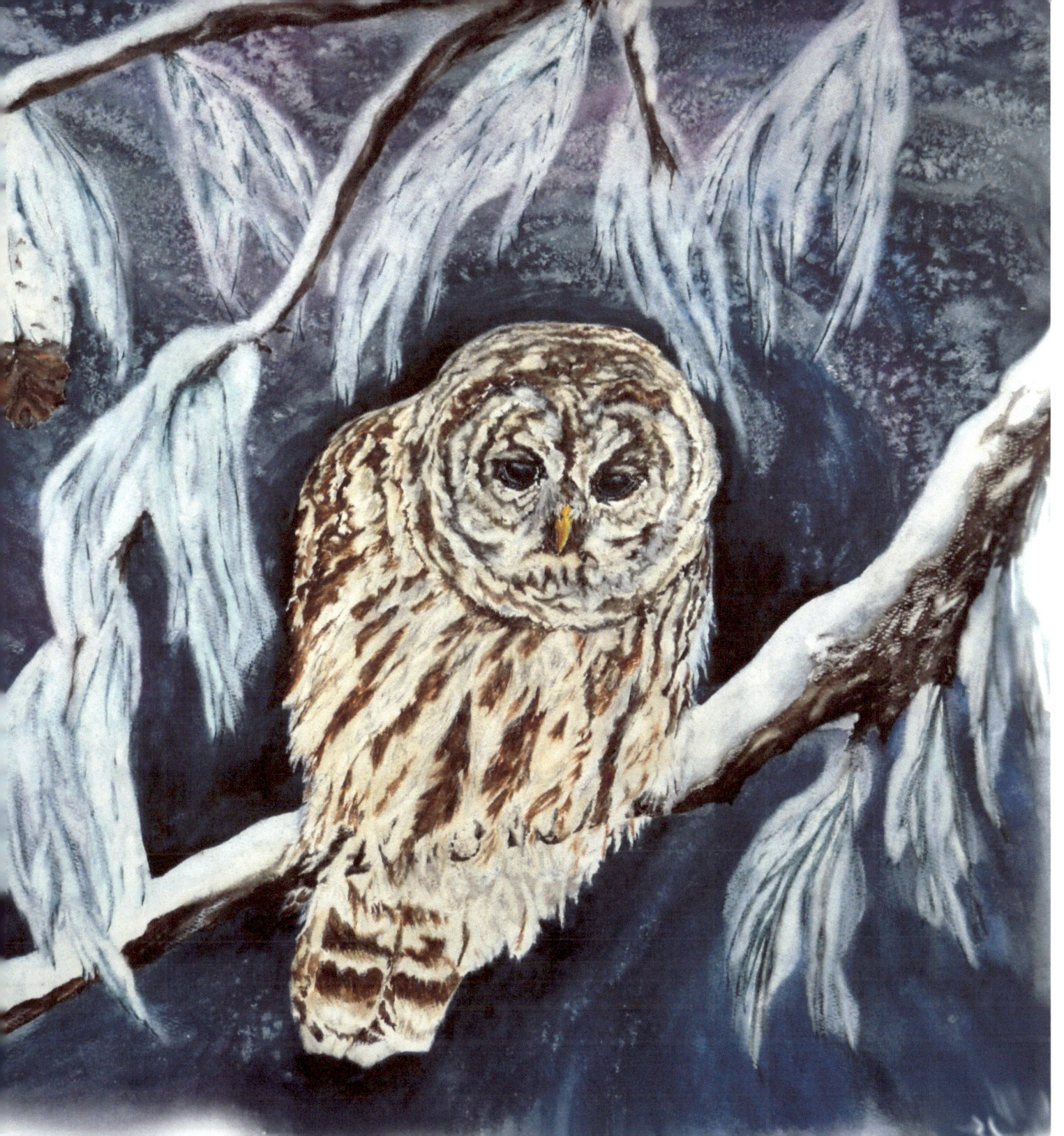

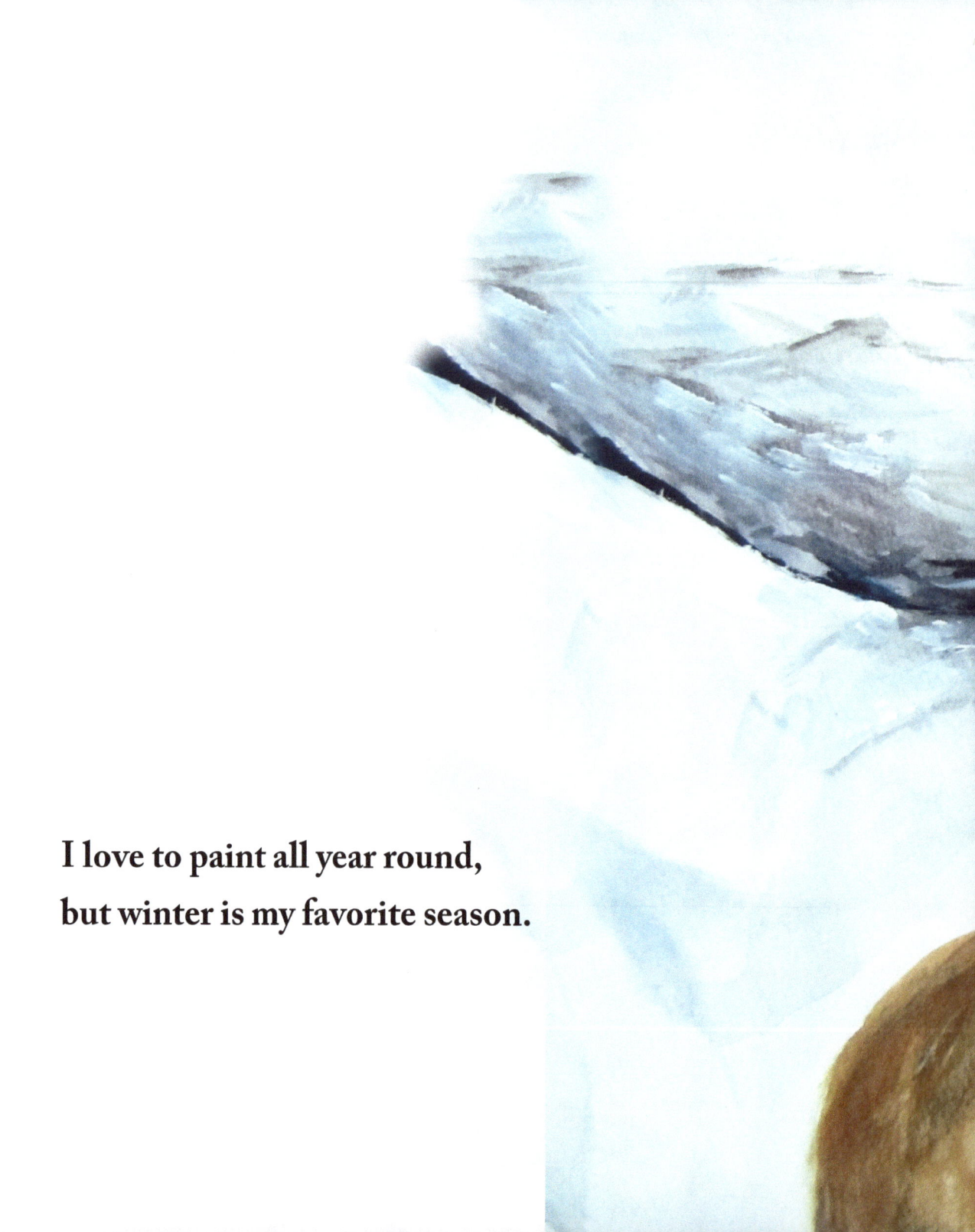

I love to paint all year round,
but winter is my favorite season.

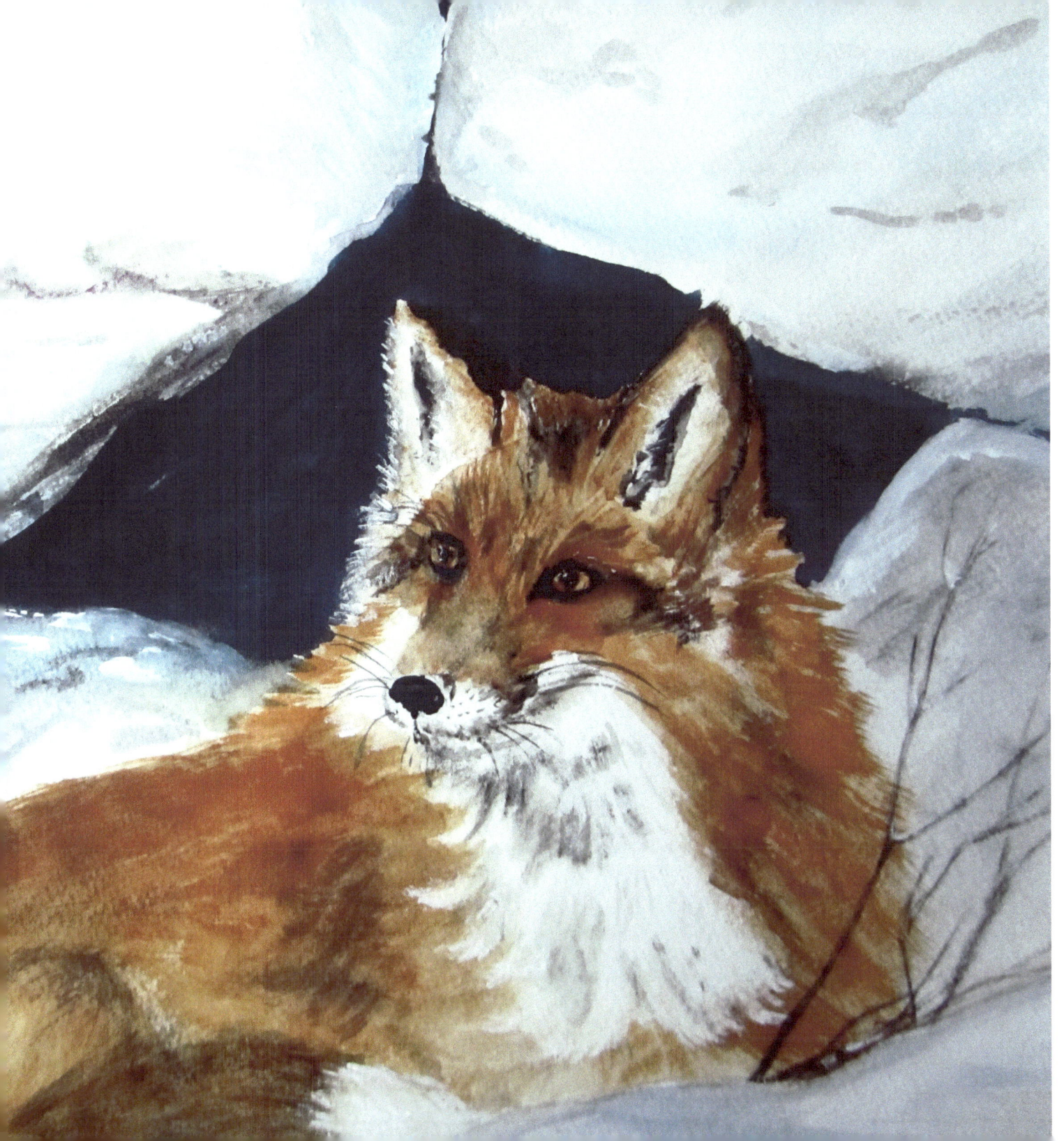

I look for animal tracks in the fresh snow.

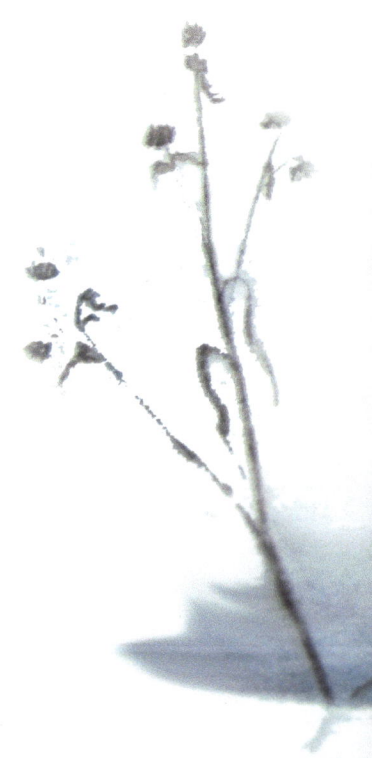

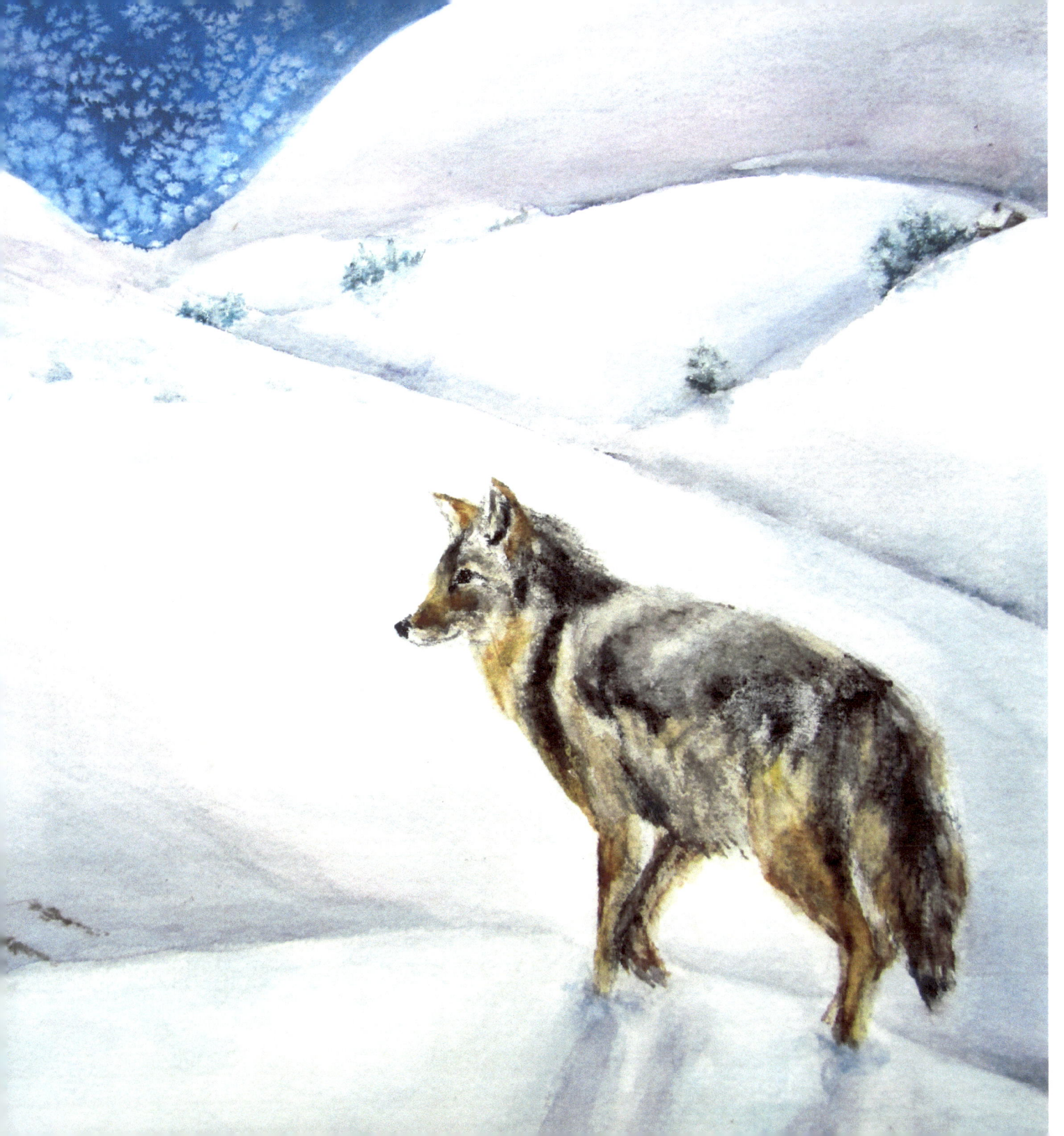

Golden eyes all keeping watch on a winter's night in the northern woods.

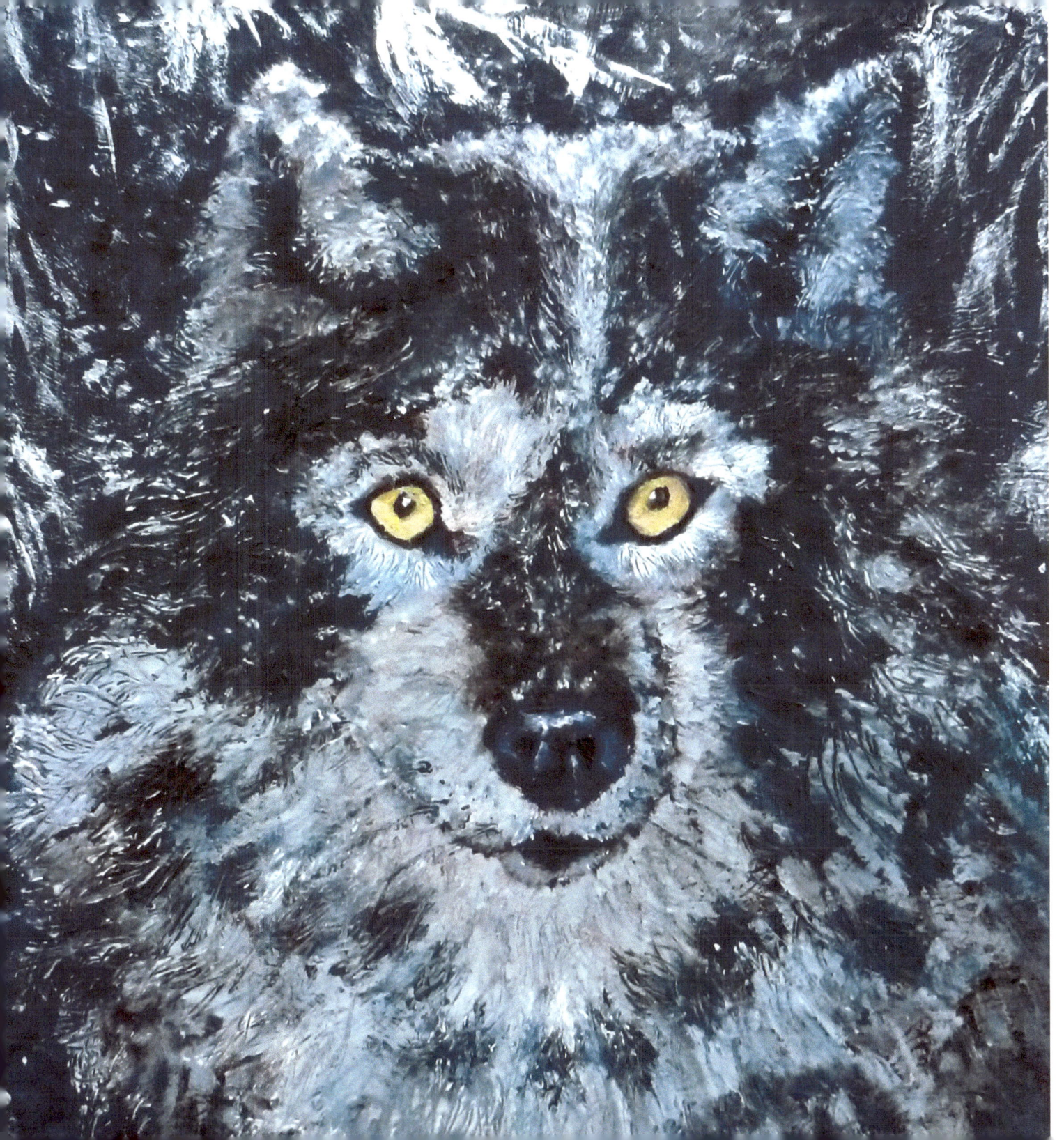

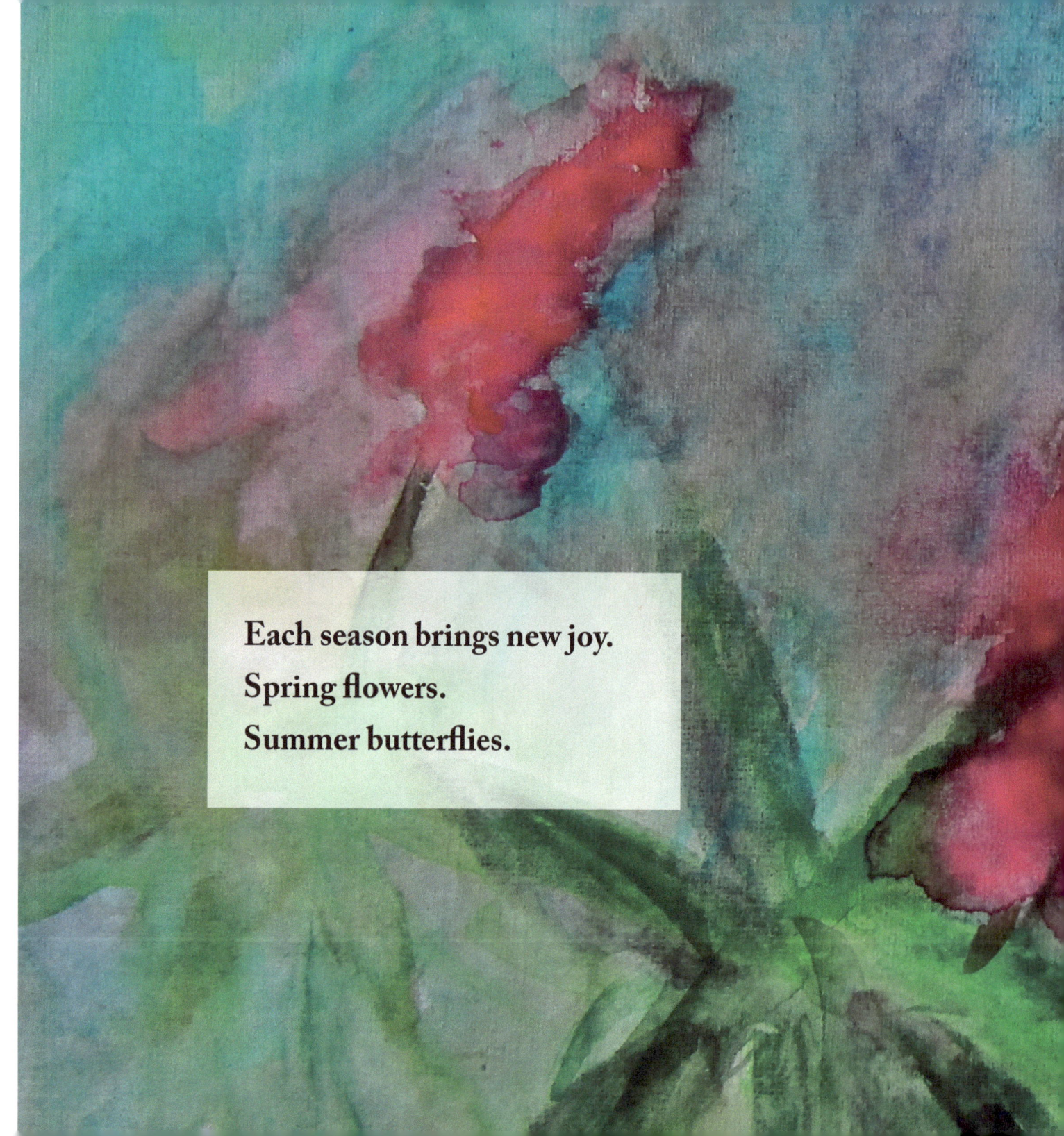

Each season brings new joy.
Spring flowers.
Summer butterflies.

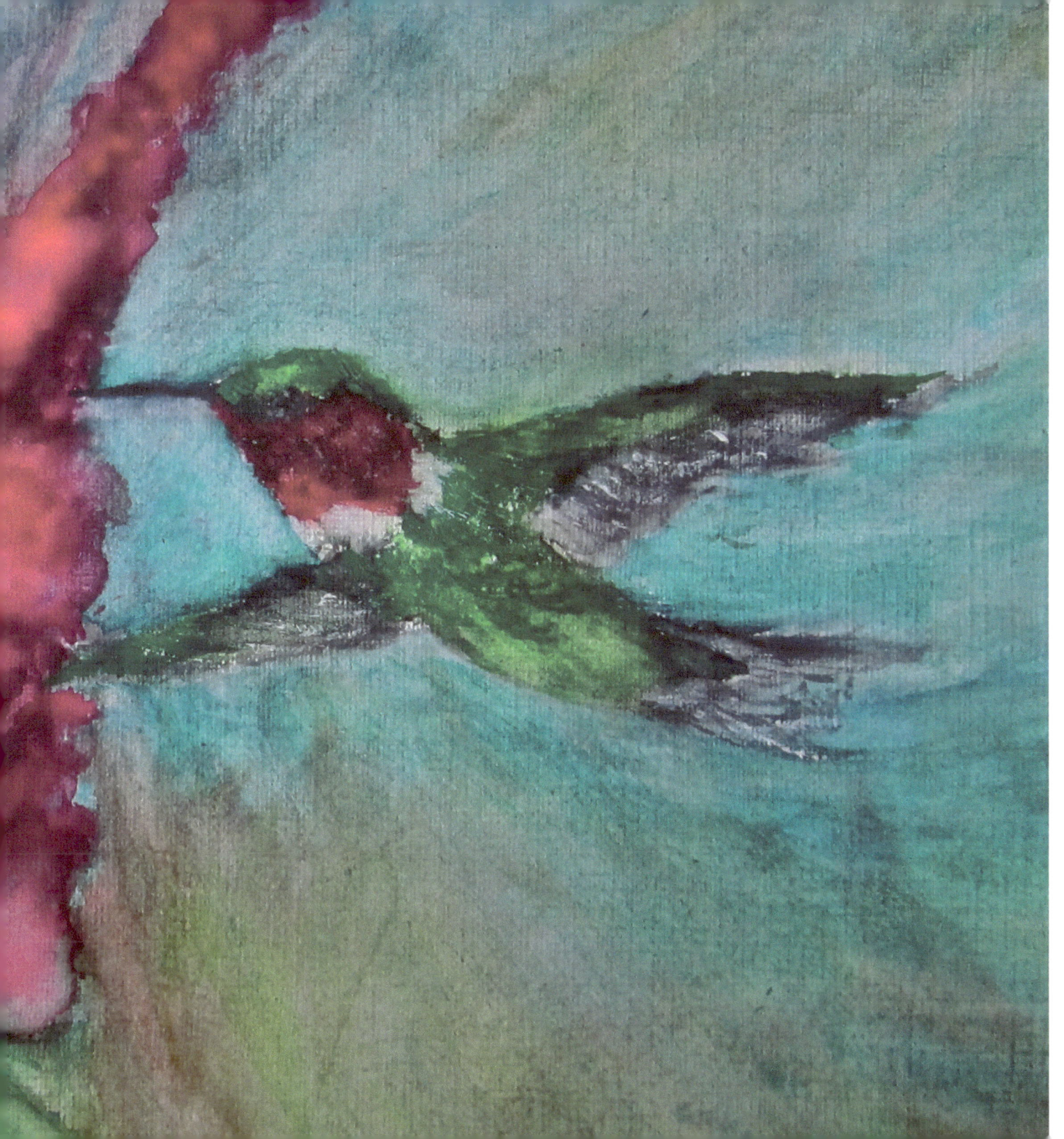

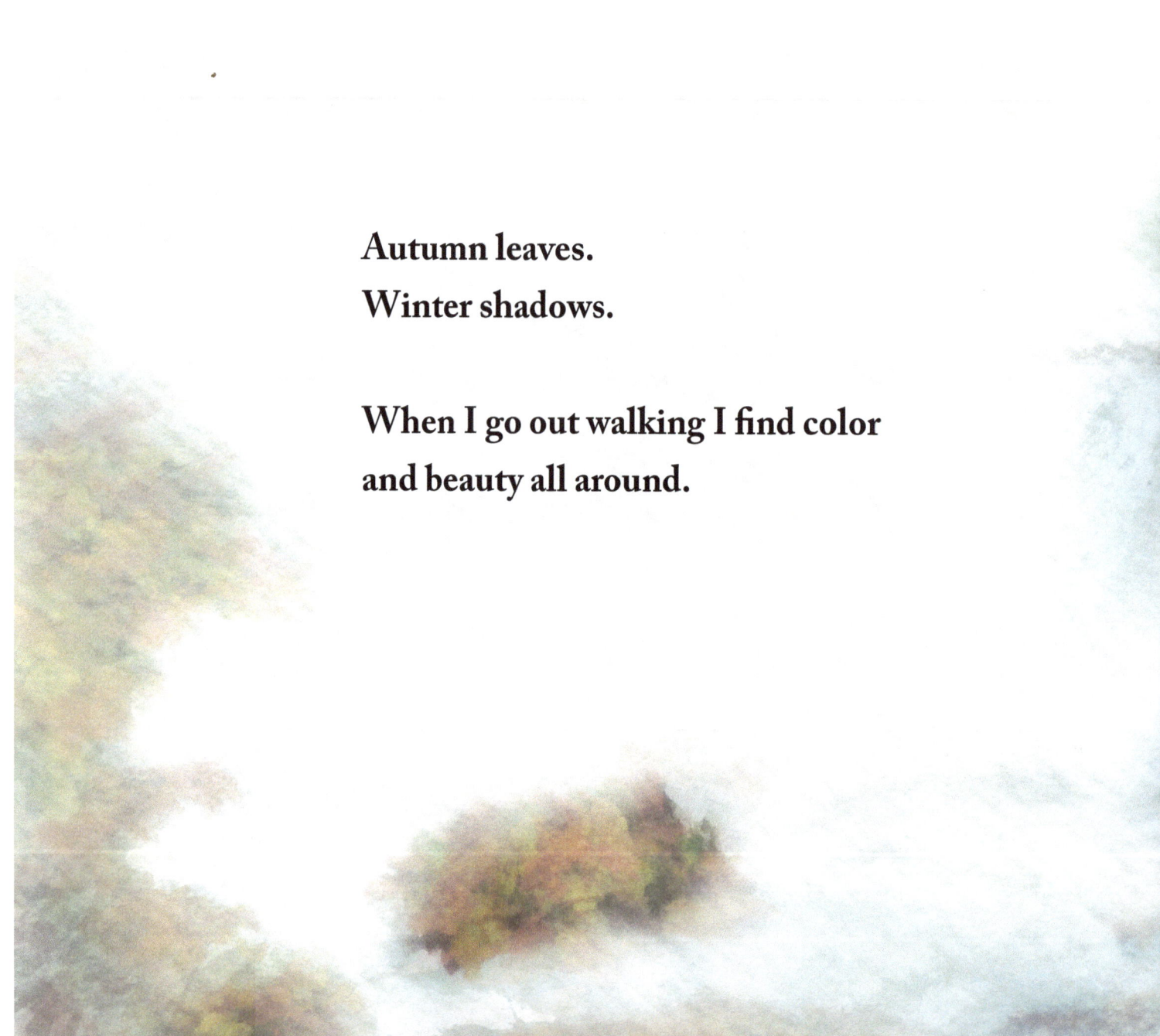

Autumn leaves.
Winter shadows.

When I go out walking I find color
and beauty all around.

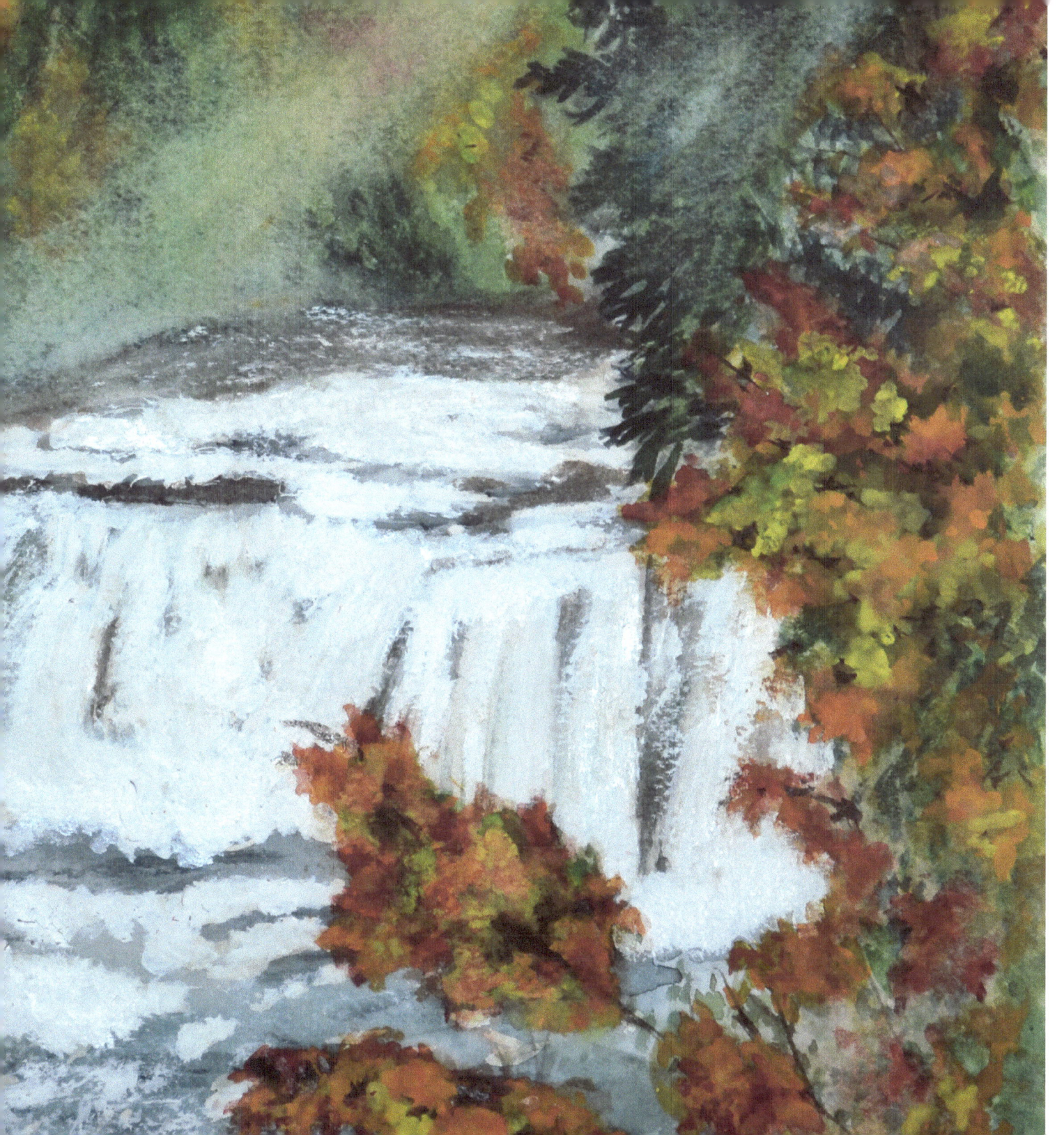

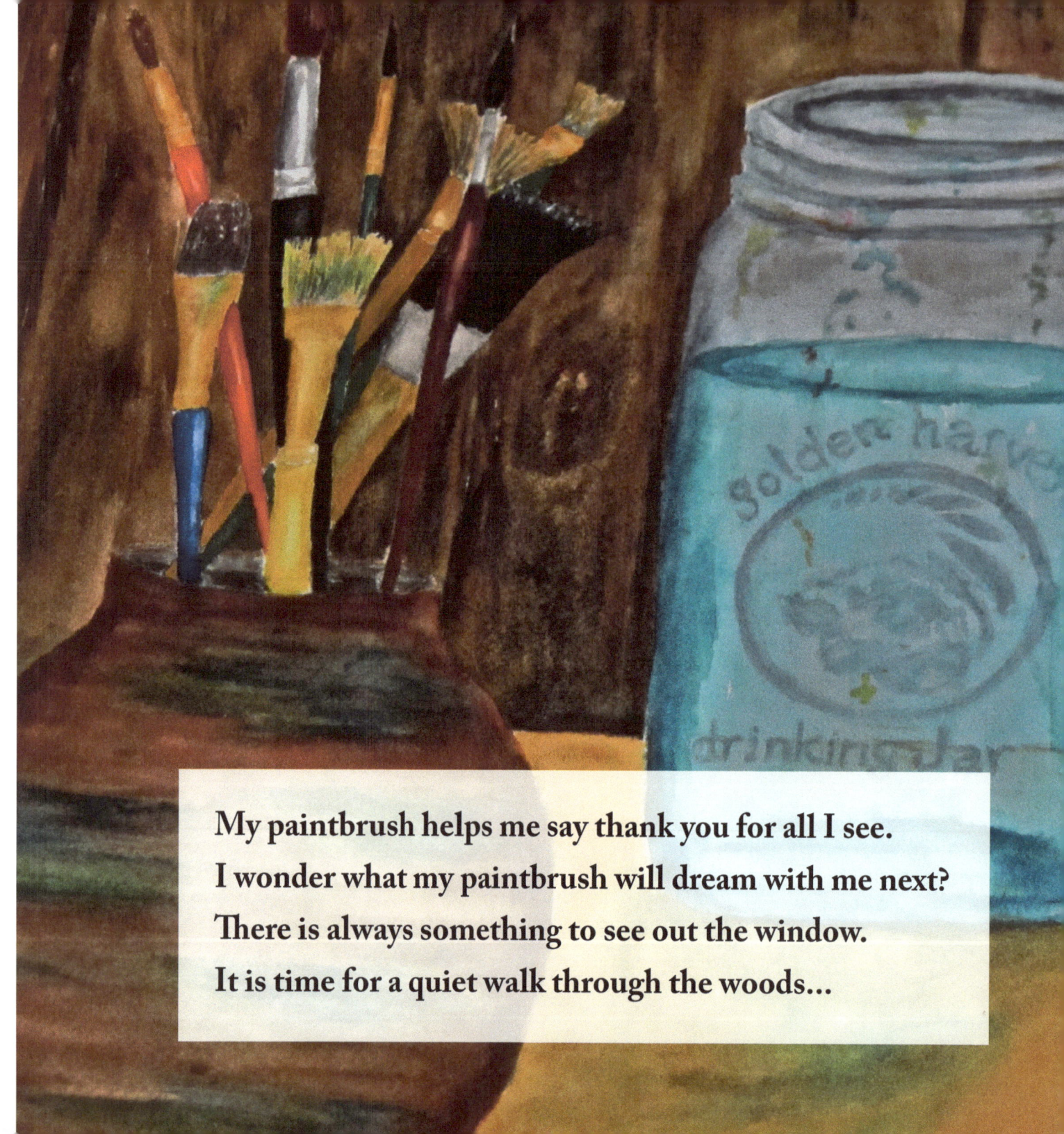

My paintbrush helps me say thank you for all I see.
I wonder what my paintbrush will dream with me next?
There is always something to see out the window.
It is time for a quiet walk through the woods...

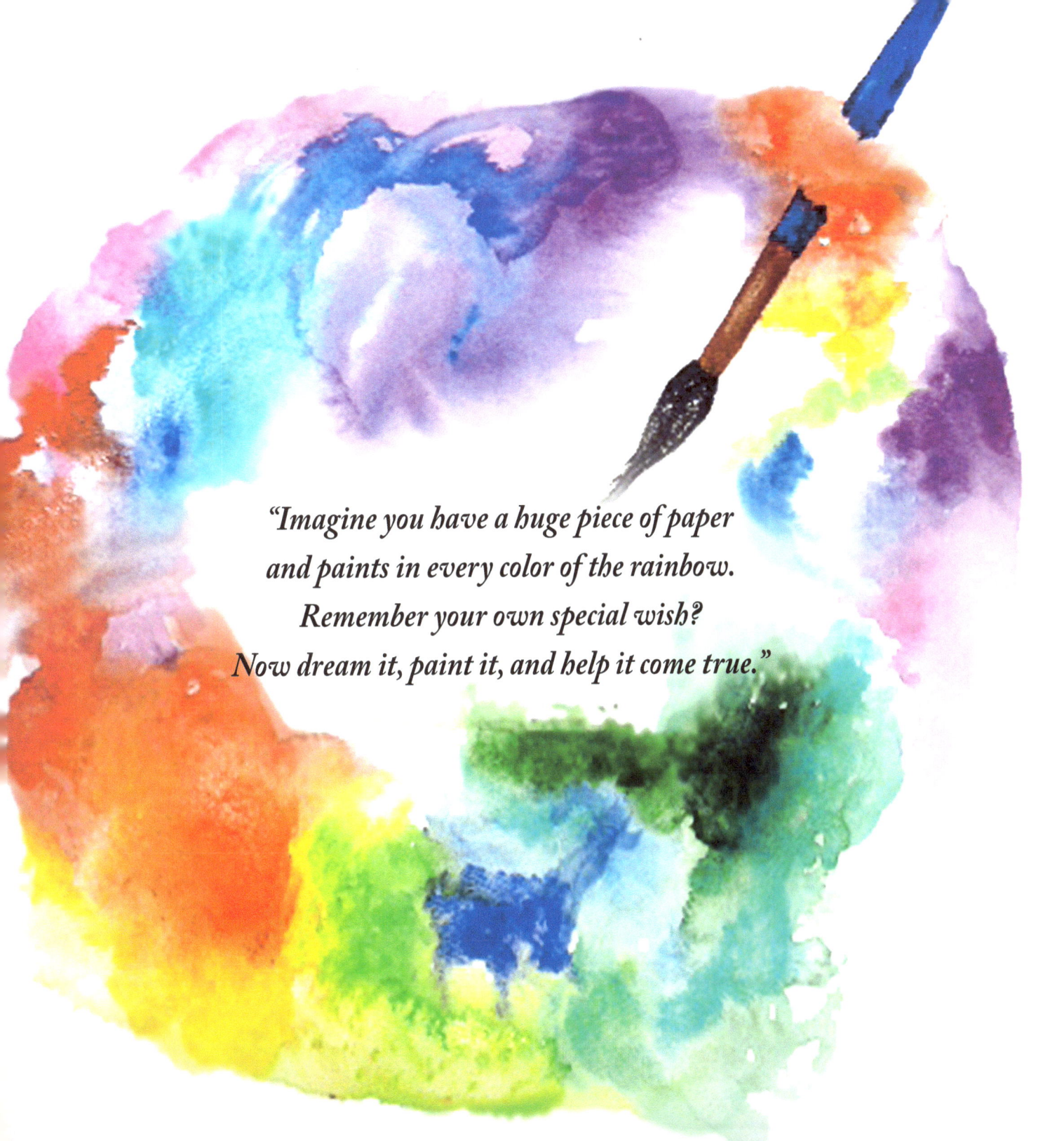

"Imagine you have a huge piece of paper
and paints in every color of the rainbow.
Remember your own special wish?
Now dream it, paint it, and help it come true."